Cuba at the crossroads

Cuba at the crossroads

Fidel Castro

OCEAN PRESS

Melbourne ◆ *New York*

ISBN 1-875284-94-X

First printed 1996

Printed in Australia

Published by Ocean Press,
GPO Box 3279, Melbourne, Victoria 3001, Australia
Fax: (61-3) 9372 1765   Email: Ocean_Press@msn.com

Ocean Press, PO Box 020692, Brooklyn, NY 11202, USA

Distributed in the United States by the Talman Company,
    131 Spring Street, New York, NY 10012, USA
Distributed in Canada by Marginal Distributors,
    277 George St. N., Unit 102, Peterborough, Ontario K9J 3G9, Canada
Distributed in Britain and Europe by Central Books,
    99 Wallis Road, London E9 5LN, Britain
Distributed in Australia by Astam Books,
    57-61 John Street, Leichhardt, NSW 2040, Australia
Distributed in Cuba and Latin America by Ocean Press,
    Apartado 686, C.P. 11300, Havana, Cuba
Distributed in Southern Africa by Phambili Agencies,
    PO Box 28680, Kensington 2101, South Africa

Contents

We want a world without hegemony, without nuclear
arms, without racism, without nationalists and religious
hatred, without outrages against the sovereignty of any
country, and with respect for peoples' independence and
free self-determination; a world without universal models
which completely fail to consider the traditions and
cultures of all the peoples that make up humanity,
without cruel blockades which kill men, women
and children, young people and old,
like silent atom bombs.

We want a world of peace, justice and dignity, in which
everybody, without any exception, has the right
to well-being and to life.

Fidel Castro to the United Nations,
October 1995

Preface

"No man is an island," wrote the poet John Donne. Yet the island of Cuba often seems, in the eyes of both its friends and foes, to be defined by one person: Fidel Castro. Student revolutionary, guerrilla commander, head of state and tireless orator, he has shared the triumphs and tribulations of the Cuban people with the world in his inspiring, amusing and informative speeches.

Barely a week goes by that the Cuban leader does not attend some conference, rally or meeting of a mass organization. He listens to the reports, discussions and debate, and then presents his views in a flowing and informal commentary that ranges from warming up the crowd with personal anecdotes to a historical discourse on the topic at hand.

Few leave these meetings early, even if the sun is hot or the rain is streaming down. Even in this day of simultaneous television broadcasts, everyone wants to be there for the speech, as close to the front as possible so they can call out comments and questions. Fidel often picks up on remarks shouted to him from the audience, so his talks are more a dialogue than a monologue.

A transcript of his speech is usually available within a day or two in *Granma*, the newspaper named for the yacht that carried Fidel and his comrades from Mexico to their rendezvous with destiny in the Sierra Maestra mountains in 1956, the beginning of the guerrilla struggle. The paper often includes comments from the audience, chants that break out, and the times he is interrupted by laughter or applause.

This form of communication with the Cuban masses and the world has no counterpart in the capitalist countries. What mechanisms do presidents of the United States, for example, have to communicate their thoughts? Only carefully scripted policy statements or campaign speeches, or "off the cuff" remarks and waves of the hand at photo ops — like the arrival of the presidential helicopter on the White House lawn.

Even presidential press conferences, or the questioning of Cabinet members by a group of journalists, have none of the democratic quality of the Cuban leader's appearances. His audiences are made up of workers of all categories, campesinos, students, solidarity brigades from other countries — whatever group has organized the event. By contrast, those who get close enough to ask questions of U.S. political leaders, especially live on television, are a carefully selected group of journalists who are generally paid six- to seven-figure salaries. And they in turn hobnob with the representatives of the very, very rich.

It is not unusual for bourgeois political figures to keep diaries during their terms of office. Many years later, when the events described are at a safe distance, their books are published with great fanfare — and substantial royalties for their authors. Both Henry Kissinger and Robert McNamara have used this literary form recently to present their version of the Vietnam War years. These works are supposed to be more candid than their public pronouncements at the time. However, despite promotional campaigns hinting that the author "tells all," their books are generally self-serving rewrites of history peppered with personal gossip.

Of course, Cuba must have its secrets, too. How could it be otherwise when its closest neighbor, the world's greatest military power, has tried ever since the Cuban revolution to bring down the government and reimpose capitalism there? Yet Fidel's speeches are amazing for their candor, their realistic and often self-critical discussion in detail of how things stand for the revolution, given all the hurdles placed before it.

And these discussions are given in the heat of the events, not at some later time when only historians and political professionals will pore over them. They are both an orientation of the populace and a public sounding board so the leaders are sure to know what the people are thinking. In many ways, they are Cuba's not-so-secret weapon in its never-ending struggle with U.S. imperialism.

At every important juncture since the revolution, Cuba's leaders have spoken to the people at mass rallies that have often swelled to a million people, out of a total population of 11 million.

And while Fidel did not speak at this year's May Day march — the largest ever — he had just delivered a major talk the day before to 2,000 union delegates at the 17th Congress of the Central Organization of Cuban Workers. This speech, which is reproduced here, honestly reviews the mixed feelings Cuba's communists have about the economic reforms. They are bringing investment and increased production into the country, and therefore a revival of the working class itself, many of whom had been idled (but not laid off) by the shortages. But they also bring a culture of personal enrichment at the expense of the collective good. Much of the congress, as reflected in this speech, was about how to get as much economic development as possible out of the reforms while counteracting their corrosive social effects.

In several of the speeches collected in this book, Fidel talks to the youth about Cuba's "special period" — the time beginning with the collapse of Eastern Europe and the Soviet Union and made much more difficult by the U.S. economic blockade. It is a hard thing, this special period. It is a time of extreme material deprivation that can only be compared to the rigors of wartime.

Most of the Cuban people today are too young to know firsthand the brutalities and misery of the Batista dictatorship that led to the 1959 revolution. What teenagers can remember is that things were much better a few years ago when they were little kids. But young Cubans have learned a high socialist morale. In the summer of 1995, they hosted youth delegations from all over the world at the "Cuba Vive" conference. In formal discussions and in thousands of rap sessions at their homes, where delegates were housed for part of the conference, they talked about the difficulties Cuba is facing and the economic measures taken by the government to survive this period. It is a measure of the great confidence Cuba's communist leaders have in the people that this event could take place at a time of so many problems. The youth themselves debated such questions as having to strengthen tourism and investment from abroad in order to revive the economy, and the harm that can do to social relations. They talked about how the new currency law legalizing dollars stimulates inequality and benefits those with relatives living abroad. None of this was swept under the rug.

In his speeches to the youth, President Fidel Castro congratulates them for taking on the big questions of the day. He goes over each workshop, noting their great concern for the future of this planet and the billions of people on it. He explains what conditions made it necessary for the revolutionary government to bring back elements of capitalism in order to survive the near collapse of its economy following the breakdown of the USSR and its allies. Most important, he talks about the political power of the people, the workers and campesinos, as the guarantor that all this will be used not just for personal gain but to strengthen the socialist institutions won by the revolution.

Visitors to Cuba — like the young people who came to the conference from hostile capitalist countries — experience culture shock when they return home. Even after a week or two in a socialist country, it is hard to go back to societies where racist violence is commonplace, where wasteful opulence and abject misery co-exist side by side, often on the same city block, and where police sirens belt out their night music.

Bourgeois journalists don't seem aware of these differences, so they make up some of their own. My favorite story on how the U.S. media handle Fidel's speeches comes from when I covered the Third Congress of the Cuban Communist Party in February 1986 for *Workers World* newspaper, the weekly organ of Workers World Party in the United States. Cuban socialist construction was in high gear then. The congress was devoted to what was called the "rectification" program: cutting back on a farmers' market that had enriched some at the expense of others, and promoting more youth, women and black Cubans to leadership positions in the Party and government.

Fidel had the responsibility of presenting the report of the Central Committee to the congress, which he did in a very detailed speech that took five hours. Most of it was written out in advance — very uncharacteristic for him — but he couldn't resist making some extemporaneous remarks. He explained that he had given up smoking his signature cigars at the request of Cuba's public health officials, who wanted him to set a healthy example for the population even though tobacco is an important Cuban export. He also joked about how U.S. President Ronald Reagan had just covered the entire State of the Union in a speech lasting about 20 minutes.

When I returned home to New York, I eagerly turned on TV to see if there was any coverage of the congress. Indeed there was: about half a minute, in which the announcer said, "Cuban dictator Fidel Castro is dying of lung cancer. He has been forced by his doctors to give up smoking and could only speak for 20 minutes at the recent

Communist Party Congress, instead of his usual marathon harangue."

When John Donne wrote that no man is an island, he meant of course that everyone is interconnected, that no person — and certainly no country — has an existence independent of the rest of human society. If this could be observed back in his day — Donne lived from 1573 to 1631 — then how much more obvious is it in this age of transnational corporations, satellite phone links and a worldwide division of labor?

The great problem facing the island of Cuba — but also its greatest strength — lies in its relationship to the ebb and flow of vast movements for social change all over the world.

The Cuban revolution has been synonymous with internationalism. Grenada, Nicaragua, Algeria, Angola, Mozambique, the African National Congress of South Africa, Ethiopia, Vietnam — all found that they were not islands either.

Cuban doctors, nurses, teachers and soldiers were ready to work, fight and die at their sides in the struggle to uproot oppressive social relations that still, in this high-tech age, prevent nations all over the world from eliminating illiteracy, infectious disease, and all the other symptoms of poverty and repression.

Last year the centennial of the death of José Martí — the immortal thinker, poet, fighter and martyr in the war for independence — was commemorated. Martí had a vision not just for Cuba but for all the Caribbean islands that shared its history of glorious struggle against slavery and colonialism.

Che Guevara, the doctor from Argentina who took up arms with Fidel against the Batista dictatorship, was the quintessential revolutionary internationalist. Once the Cuban revolution had been secured, Che carried the skill, experience and authority he had earned there to Africa and finally to Bolivia, where he was assassinated while fighting agents of the CIA.

How the empire builders in Washington wish they could just sink the whole island of Cuba! On a U.S. plane once I found a tourist magazine with a map of the Caribbean that looked odd, somehow. It took me a moment to realize that Cuba had simply vanished. Where the island shaped like a great bird's wing should have been were little wavy blue lines representing the sea.

This mentality reflects how they have tried every trick in the book to isolate Cuba. Whatever they are called — the Torricelli "Cuban Democracy" Act, the Helms-Burton Act — the anti-Cuba laws penned in Washington are meant to dry up the lifeblood of commerce that every nation depends on to survive in the modern era.

But socialist Cuba has survived. Despite all the predictions of its imminent downfall. Despite the rush a few years ago — led by President George Bush's son Jeb — to set up a $10 billion corporation that would cash in when the revolutionary government was overthrown and Cuba's factories, stores, offices, farms, hospitals and hotels were returned to private ownership.

Cuba remains a country where the people have the power. And in the words of Fidel Castro to the "Cuba Vive" youth conference, "While the people have the power, they have everything."

There was a time 35 years ago when it seemed as though the economic noose U.S. imperialism was tightening around Cuba could not but strangle the exuberance, the daring to hope, the wild and often hilarious energy released by the revolution. After all, Cuba was a small country, just 90 miles from Florida. How could it incur the intense wrath of Wall Street and survive?

The crunch came in June 1960 when U.S. oil companies in Cuba refused to refine cheaper Soviet oil, the first such shipment to Cuba. That was telling the Cubans to accept Washington's dictates or be forced to their knees economically. It was the decisive act in a long series of war-like moves that tested the Cuban leaders' resolve.

Even as a U.S. aircraft carrier sailed past Havana, two of its jets buzzing the refineries, the Cuban government announced it was taking the plants over and would refine the oil itself.

The international implications were enormous. Cuba was not alone. Even if Washington were to bludgeon almost all the countries of Latin America into joining its anti-Cuba blockade — which did happen — the revolution had allies among the socialist countries.

Fidel Castro has cited in speech after speech the importance of the international solidarity the Cuban people received over the years from the USSR and other socialist countries. It was a strong material factor in Cuba's ability to survive the economic blockade and awesome military threats emanating from the U.S. government.

In all the organs of propaganda that serve the capitalist foreign-policy establishment, the United States was presented as the aggrieved party. Here we were so friendly to the Cuban revolutionaries, the story went, welcoming their overthrow of the Batista dictatorship. But they had to turn around and bite the hand that fed them by aligning with the enemy: communism. This is still the view presented by the Cuban right wing and its patrons in the United States.

Yet even books like *Fidel: A Critical Portrait* by *New York Times* reporter Tad Szulc admit that long before the revolutionary leaders had even mentioned any socialist measures for Cuba, the U.S. government had decided to overthrow them. On March 10, 1959 — barely 10 weeks after the victory over Batista — the National Security Council held a secret meeting to discuss how to bring "another government to power in Cuba."

On the surface, the Eisenhower administration appeared to have a measured attitude toward Cuba. In reality the CIA was gearing up a campaign of propaganda and terrorist attacks against the popular revolutionary government.

What made them and their Democrat successors hate the revolution so much? The hostility of the U.S. ruling class crystallized with the May 17, 1959, signing of Cuba's agrarian reform law. It limited most land ownership to 966 acres per individual; sugar, rice and cattle farms could be as big as 3,300 acres.

U.S. companies had owned the best agricultural land in Cuba. Their holdings were enormous: one spread covered 480,000 acres. Although the agrarian reform law promised payment for what was nationalized, they knew their lucrative exploitation of Cuba's resources had come to an end.

And the Cubans meant business. INRA (National Institute for Agrarian Reform), the ministry set up to enforce the agrarian reform, began organizing a powerful militia of workers and peasants. For Cuba's rural population — many of them landless agricultural workers who had slaved in the fields during the four-month-long sugar harvest and starved the rest of the year — this was true empowerment.

Whether they had knowledge of the National Security Council's agenda, Cuba's leaders certainly knew what was happening when a campaign of right-wing sabotage began. Theaters and shops were bombed. A ship was blown up in Havana harbor. Counterrevolutionary guerrilla bands began operating in the Escambray mountains. This was followed by an all-out invasion of U.S.-trained mercenaries at the Bay of Pigs in 1961 and a nuclear crisis with the United States in 1962.

Yet Cuba moved ahead — with land reform, with an unprecedented mass literacy campaign, with building mass organizations of women, youths, workers, neighborhood associations and a people's militia.

At the height of the Bay of Pigs invasion, Fidel Castro announced to the world for the first time that Cuba had made a socialist revolution "under the very noses of the Yankee imperialists." Far from being shocked at this information, the Cuban people responded by fighting the invaders even harder. I was in the New York office of the July 26 Movement when Fidel's speech was broadcast over shortwave. The Cuban workers who had packed in to hear it shouted, threw their berets in the air and hugged as their leader pronounced his fateful words. Cuba would never go back to being a colony of U.S. sugar interests.

Cuba's leaders have remained faithful to this socialist objective, even though the intervening years have shown that the struggle is a longer and harder one than could have been envisioned at that time.

In his speech on the 35th anniversary of Cuba's victory at the Bay of Pigs — included in this book — Fidel returned to a favorite theme: the teachings of José Martí on the struggle for independence. "Our independence requires struggle and sacrifice," said Fidel. "Our dignity, our honor, our right to progress, our tomorrow, our future — everything they want to take away from us costs dearly. But all of us, men and women, boys and girls, all of us who have had the privilege of feeling pride, dignity and honor... are determined to pay the price, because we will never resign ourselves to living without them."

Until the collapse of Eastern Europe and the USSR, Cuba was a member of Comecon[1] — an association of states with planned

---

[1] Comecon, the Council of Mutual Economic Assistance (also referred to as CMEA), was the economic union of the Soviet Union, the Eastern European socialist countries and Mongolia to coordinate economic trade and assistance. Cuba joined Comecon in July 1972.

economies that did not follow the profit-driven dictates of the world capitalist market. During these years of socialist construction, Cuba made enormous advances in health care, education, culture, sports, housing — all the areas most affecting the lives of the masses. For more than three decades, Cubans have lived without the daily humiliations and bitter taste that come with having to serve a boss or a landlord.

The most basic human right — the right to be treated as an equal — is now deeply rooted in Cuba's social soil.

But the collapse of the Soviet Union and its allies in Eastern Europe has taken an enormous toll. A decline of 70 percent in Cuba's imports affected not only individual consumption but agricultural and industrial production. This made it imperative that Cuba find new means to carry out trade and commerce with the world, especially with the capitalist economies.

Progressives everywhere have held their breath, knowing that when the imperialists get an inch they want a mile. Yet this special period has demonstrated the great inner strength and resilience of the new socialist order.

Despite hardships that would long ago have brought down any capitalist government in the world, the revolutionary Cuban people have weathered the storm with their political power intact. And though Cubans must still wear tight belts, the economic situation has begun to turn around. Output figures are now rising, not falling. Despite President Bill Clinton's signing of the Helms-Burton bill expanding the U.S. blockade, Cuba is widening its commerce and ties with the rest of the world.

Helms-Burton, in fact, will prove a thorn in the side of U.S. capitalism. Already, it has deeply angered countries all over the world for trying to superimpose U.S. law on their commercial activities. In an unprecedented act of independence, the Organization of American States voted nearly unanimously — the U.S. delegate cast the lone dissenting vote — to condemn it. Canada and Mexico are contesting it as a violation of the North American Free Trade Agreement. Britain, France and other European countries are taking it to the World Court.

Cuba's decision to vigorously defend its sovereign territory and shoot down an invading plane on February 24, 1996, has not had the dire effects that some predicted. It put the counterrevolutionaries on notice that their mercenary relation with the North American godfathers is no guarantee of impunity.

When this was followed by a meeting of the Cuban Communist Party's Central Committee that laid out measures to counteract the harmful social effects of some of the economic reforms, the message was made doubly clear: there has been no change in the socialist orientation of Cuba's leadership or of the masses. And to deflate further any hopes the imperialists may have had that years of sacrifice would wear down the working class, this year's May Day parade in Havana was the largest ever — 1.3 million.

This is good news not only for Cuba but for the whole world movement.

Today more than ever, the world's people need to shake off the tyranny of big capital that stands between technological development and humanity's social progress. What good are today's labor-saving miracles if all they bring are massive unemployment and insecurity? What good are green revolutions in agriculture if they force impoverished peasants off the land to become even more impoverished urban squatters?

Socialism means breaking the blockade of private monopoly ownership of the means of production. Cuba has shown that even under the most difficult conditions, a socialist state drawing on the political power of the masses can quickly solve problems that are seen as intractable in the richest capitalist countries — problems like racism, illiteracy, malnutrition, homelessness, drug abuse and alienation.

"The more Cuba resists, the more it is respected," said Fidel Castro in his speech to the youth, "and Cuba is ready to win the respect of the whole world." Cuba belongs to the world. No efforts to isolate it can keep its example from taking wing and bringing hope that both resistance and victory are possible.

Deirdre Griswold
Editor
Workers World newspaper
New York, June 1996

World Solidarity Conference

Speech of November 25, 1994

President Fidel Castro delivered this speech at the closing session of the first World Solidarity with Cuba Conference, held in the Karl Marx Theater in Havana, on November 25, 1994. Attending the conference, which took place November 21–25, were 3,072 delegates from 109 countries on five continents, who came to Cuba to discuss how to increase political and material solidarity with Cuba. In addition to adopting a program of action against the U.S. blockade, the assembly declared 1995 as the International Year of José Martí, in honor of the centennial of Martí's death.[1]

It is difficult to summarize or make a synthesis of the contents of these conference days, but I can make some comments. Through-out the last few days we have heard the best sentiments and the best ideas of this century, expressed as a call to battle, you could say. We have discussed many aspects arising from humanity's concerns over many years. In one way or another, you have expressed values for which humanity has battled and fought through-out this century, now drawing to a close.

---

[1] José Martí, Cuba's national hero, revolutionary leader and poet, wrote extensively about his views of a liberated Cuba. He was killed fighting for Cuba's independence from Spain on May 19, 1895.

Throughout this conference, you have discussed the issues central to the long-fought struggles for independence and against colonialism, neocolonialism and imperialism. The fight by the world's peoples for equality, for justice, for their development, for their sovereignty, never so threatened as today. The fight for social justice, the fight against exploitation, the fight against poverty, the fight against ignorance, the fight against disease, the fight for all vulnerable and dispossessed peoples, the fight for dignity, the fight for respect for women, the fight for unity among all peoples and races, the fight for peace — all of these values and many more. Thus we could say that this has not just been a conference of solidarity with Cuba, and it fills us with pride that this solidarity has inspired such a discussion.

The best values of our time have been reflected at this meeting, and we have also seen the presence of many, though not all — for there are so many that they would never fit into 1,000 or 10,000 theaters such as this one — of the world's finest, most selfless and altruistic citizens, representatives of humanity's best. This meeting has been attended by persons with the highest human and moral sensibility. I greatly admire humankind's capacity to give, to sacrifice, to show generosity. Absent from this meeting are many, many people whom we know as friends, who have demonstrated their solidarity and who have been examples of sensitivity, solidarity and human generosity. But those traits remain the indelible, unforgettable impression that we will take away with us from this conference.

How has this conference unfolded and developed? Everyone I have talked with has told me it has gone well. It has been unlike many of the other conferences we have had, where everyone who wanted to speak did so and the meetings became an interminable series of speeches. Although this meeting has witnessed many excellent, brilliant, profound and cogent speeches, an event many days longer and dedicated to letting everyone speak would not have had the same quality.

Thus there have been speeches, statements from the floor, questions and answers; we have had the working commissions on various themes. Those who did not speak here spoke there, and a miracle has been worked to allow contributions from hundreds of people, although it was impossible for everyone to speak.

I think that the people who did speak more or less expressed the sentiments of everyone present. For that reason, we have to congratulate the organizers and leaders of this event, since in spite of differences, we have not had a Tower of Babel, and despite language diversity — 109 countries are represented here, according to the information given out — we have understood each other perfectly well because, although we have different languages and even different political opinions, we were unanimous in the noble idea of solidarity with the Cuban people.

What is the blockade?

The blockade has become the central issue of this event. Many people have talked on this subject; comrades have stated that there is nothing much to add about the blockade. But what is the blockade? The blockade is not only the prohibition by the United States of any kind of trade with our country, whether it is technology, machinery; whether it is something more, food; whether it is medicine. The blockade means that they cannot sell to Cuba even an aspirin to relieve a headache, or an anti-cancer drug that could save lives or alleviate the suffering of the terminally ill. Nothing, absolutely nothing can be sold to Cuba!

The blockade is not only the prohibition of all credits and finance facilities. The blockade is not only the total closure of economic, commercial and financial activities by the United States, the world's richest nation, the most powerful nation of the world in economic and military terms. It is not only just 90 miles off our coasts, but a few inches away from us, in the occupied territory of the Guantánamo Naval Base.

The most powerful imperialist nation is not only close to us, but within Cuba. And it is not only close to us with its ideas, its theories, its concepts, its philosophy, but it is also among us in that minority that unfortunately supports the concepts, philosophy and ideas they have been disseminating for so many years throughout the world.

The United States does not trade with markets that trade with Cuba, but it does want to export ideas, and the worst ideas. It does not export foodstuffs to Cuba, it does not export medicines, technology or machinery to Cuba, but it does export incredible quantities of ideas. What is happening now is that before the ideas market was much wider, and it exported many ideas to the socialist bloc, to the former Soviet Union and other countries. These days the United States reserves its counterrevolutionary ideas for us, from a vast and powerful stock of enormous, infinite mass-media programming. This trade is a one-way trade as we do not have that kind of mass media, those enormous communications systems which cost billions, tens of billions of dollars every year, which we are condemned to receive, not to exchange.

The blockade is economic war

But the blockade is not only that. The blockade is an economic war waged against Cuba, an economic war. It is the tenacious, constant persecution of any Cuban economic deal made anywhere in the world. The United States actively operates, through its diplomatic channels, through its embassies, to put pressure on any country that wishes to trade with Cuba; or any business interest wishing to make commercial links with or invest in Cuba; to pressure and punish any boat transporting cargo to Cuba. It is a universal war, with an immense balance of power in its favor, against the economy of our country, going to the extreme of taking action against individuals who attempt to undertake any economic activity with our country.

They euphemistically refer to it as an embargo. We call it a blockade, but it is not an embargo or a blockade — it's war! A war solely and exclusively waged against Cuba and against no other country in the world.

We have not only had to endure the blockade during the years of the revolution. We have also had to endure incessant hostility in the political sphere, from attempts to eliminate the revolution's leaders, through every known form of subversion and destabilization, to direct and perennial sabotage of our economy.

During the last 35 years, we have been the victims of every kind of sabotage. I am not just referring to piracy, mercenary invasion, dirty wars in the mountains and the plains, consistent and widespread destabilization attempts, but we have also been the victims of direct sabotage involving explosives and incendiary devices.

Our country has also been subject to chemical warfare, through the introduction of toxic elements, and biological warfare via the introduction of plant, animal and human diseases. There are no weapons or resources that have not been used against our country and our revolution by U.S. authorities and governments.

But you don't have to take my word for it. From time to time documents appear, papers that have been declassified after 25 years, although there are others that are kept for 50 or 100 years. Some say they hold them back for 200 years, something for the grandchildren or the great-grandchildren or great-great-grandchildren of the current generation, who will one day learn about the barbarities which these "champions" of freedom, these "champions" of human rights have committed. The war waged against the Cuban revolution has been total and absolute. And it is not an old war; it is still being maintained, and plans are being made and carried out to sabotage our economy and our strategic industries.

Currently, organizations closely linked to the U.S. government are preparing to attack the revolution's leaders. Nobody should think that this is a thing of the past; it's going on right now. They are planning dirty wars, armed mercenary infiltrations to kill, sabotage, create insecurity, and to bring death to every part of our country. I am saying this in all seriousness, that such actions against Cuba are being planned by the United States. This amounts to something more, much more, than an economic blockade.

All these policies come accompanied by an incessant defamation and slander campaign against our country, as a justification for their crimes. Now the fundamental emphasis is being put on the human rights banner. Human rights are being quoted by those people who have committed and are committing all kinds of atrocities against our country.

As I recently stated to the United Nations High Commissioner for Human Rights, with whom I conversed at length, the most brutal and cruel violation of the human rights of our people is being committed with the purpose of killing off 11 million Cubans or bringing them to their knees through hunger and disease!

The United States: the "champion" of human rights

The United States talking about human rights! They began by exterminating their earliest indigenous or native population. Who could forget that period and that tradition of collecting the scalps of

American Indians? They killed more American Indians than buffalo, and they even finished off the buffalo.

They expanded their country at the cost of other territories; they extended their country by grabbing land, thus dispossessing their neighbors, in one way or another, of millions of square kilometers of land. In terms of Mexico alone, they grabbed over half of its territory. They still occupy Puerto Rico. They have wanted to devour Cuba for over 150 years. They have intervened dozens of times in Latin American countries. They imposed a canal in Panama. This refers just to our hemisphere. I have not mentioned the wars in Vietnam, Laos, Cambodia, and in many other places.

What a history! And what a paradox that they have just approved Proposition 187[2] — this was not 100 years ago, nor 100 days ago, but just a few weeks ago — to bar health care and education for undocumented children, for those families living in what was once Mexican territory.

What respect for human rights is shown by these concepts? What ideas, what concepts about human beings? It's inconceivable that a child could fall ill and not be treated, when $300 billion are spent on the military budget and on the most sophisticated weapons ever known.

We don't have to look back in history. In contemporary times, since the start of the revolution, what has been the history of the foreign policy of the United States, that "champion" of freedom, that "champion" of human rights? A close alliance with the most repressive and bloody regimes in the world.

If we turn to Europe, we can recall that immediately after World War I the United States became the ally of Spanish fascism, which was supplied with weapons from Hitler and Mussolini and which cost millions of lives.

We cannot overlook the U.S. alliance with South Vietnam and its genocidal war against the Vietnamese people in the south and north of that country. We cannot overlook the Korean War, because

---

[2] California's Proposition 187, which passed in the 1994 elections amidst a rightwing, racist campaign against immigrants, bars undocumented individuals from receiving any but emergency medical services, and prohibits undocumented children from receiving a public education. To date, implementation has been blocked by legal challenges to the law's constitutionality.

Korea was completely demolished, reduced to dust. We cannot ignore Hiroshima and Nagasaki and the unnecessary use of nuclear weapons — a completely unnecessary use and which, in any event, could have been used against military installations, but which fell on civilian populations of hundreds of thousands of inhabitants. It rang in the era of atomic terror in the world.

We cannot forget the alliance with South Africa and apartheid. Neither can we forget that the apartheid regime built its own nuclear weapons, and when we were fighting in southern Angola against the apartheid army, alongside the Angolans, South Africa already had nuclear weapons, various nuclear weapons! The United States knew that South Africa had nuclear weapons and that those nuclear weapons could have been used against Cuban and Angolan soldiers. Ah! But this was the South Africa of racism and fascism.

The United States has created a great fuss and has even threatened war against North Korea, due to its assumption that the North Koreans were developing nuclear weaponry. But it tolerated, allowed and indirectly facilitated South Africa's building of nuclear weapons.

But if we come closer to our continent, and to recent times, who could forget the dirty war in Nicaragua, orchestrated via armed mercenaries, which cost tens of thousands of lives and the mutilation of thousands and thousands of Nicaraguans? Who could forget that? The "champion" of freedom! The "champion" of human rights!

Who could forget the dirty war in El Salvador, the U.S. government support for a genocidal government to which it gave billions of dollars in sophisticated weapons to trample on the people's rebellion, a war that caused over 50,000 deaths?

And why did the Malvinas War happen?[3] Simply because the United States had been using Argentina's 401st special forces battalion for its dirty war against Nicaragua and El Salvador, and it provided such exceptional service to the United States that the battalion felt it could occupy the Malvinas Islands.

This has nothing to do with Argentina's right to the Malvinas, which we have always defended. But the Argentine military felt that the moment had come to collect from the United States for services

---

[3] The Malvinas War was fought in 1982 between Argentina and Great Britain over control of the Islas Malvinas (Falkland Islands) — Argentinian territory located off its coast — that is colonized by the British.

rendered in Central America, so that the former would back them in their military adventure. It was an adventure, in fact, because in the final analysis that is not the way to wage war. You either wage war or you don't. And if you wage war, you take it to its ultimate consequences if it's a just war. And they invaded the Malvinas Islands. But when the United States was put into the position of choosing between its allies and its British forebears, they chose and backed the British.

Who can forget what has happened in Guatemala since Arbenz's government in the 1950s, when a popular government chosen by the people was trying to carry out agrarian reform to help campesinos and indigenous communities?[4] Immediately the dirty war broke out and they were invaded by mercenaries. And what has happened since then? What has happened up until now? More than 100,000 people have disappeared. This is a country where for decades there were no political prisoners because everyone disappeared.

To this day, who supplies this government, who trains it, who prepares it? The "champion" of freedom, the "champion" of human rights.

And what happened in Chile with Salvador Allende's government, which had great popular support?[5] They plotted against him. The economy was blocked in many ways and conditions were gradually created for a coup, which gave the country thousands and thousands of disappeared persons and murders.

And what happened in Argentina with that military government I mentioned? They say at least 15,000 disappeared. [The audience tells him "30,000!"] I say "at least," because I don't want people to think I'm exaggerating, and yet many say there were 30,000, and

---

[4] In June 1954, the CIA succeeded in ousting Jacobo Arbenz Guzmán, president of Guatemala, through the "rebel army" it had trained and supported. United Fruit (later United Brands and Chiquita Brands) had also played a major role in the overthrow to combat Arbenz's efforts at agrarian reform.

[5] Chile's democratically elected president, Salvador Allende (1908–73), was murdered in a CIA-masterminded military coup on September 11, 1973. Allende was head of the Popular Unity government, which carried out a program of social reforms and nationalization of Chile's resources and foreign companies. The CIA and such U.S. corporations as Anaconda Copper and ITT had been actively working to overthrow him since before he took office in October 1970.

some people here are saying even more. But let's take my figures as the minimum. Are 15,000 disappeared really a small number?

And who provided weapons to this government, who backed it, who gave it political support, who made use of their services in Central America? The "champions" of freedom, the "champions" of human rights!"

And what happened in Uruguay? And what happened in Brazil? And who supported the coup leaders and those who tortured and killed people and made them disappear? Who invaded the Dominican Republic at the time of the Caamaño rebellion? Who invaded Grenada? Who invaded Panama? The "champions" of freedom and human rights!

Which of those governments was harassed? Which of the governments I named have been blockaded? Which of them have been denied credit and trade? Which were denied the purchase of weapons and war matériel? Whom didn't they train in so-called anti-subversive action? Whom didn't they train in the arts of crime, disappearances and torture? And these are the ones who blockade Cuba, who slander Cuba, who accuse Cuba of human rights violations to justify their crimes against our people.

And I can say dispassionately, without being subjective, that Cuba is the country that has done the most for human beings.

Principles of the Cuban revolution

What revolution was more noble? What revolution was more generous? What revolution showed most respect for people? And I'm not only talking about a victorious revolution in power, but since the time of our own war, of our own revolutionary struggle, which established inviolable principles. What made us revolutionaries was rejection of injustice, the rejection of crime and the rejection of torture. During the 25 months that our intense war lasted, in which we captured thousands of prisoners, there was not one case of physical violence to obtain information, not even in the midst of the war; there was not one case of killing a prisoner. What we would do with prisoners is set them free. We would keep their weapons, which was all we were interested in, and we treated these arms suppliers with all the consideration they deserved.

At first they had been led to believe that we would kill them all, and in fact they would resist up to the bitter end. But when they discovered during the course of the war the true behavior of the Rebel Army, they would give up their weapons with less of a struggle when they were surrounded, when they knew they had lost. Some of those soldiers surrendered three times, because they were switched from one front to the other and they were used to surrendering, they had experience.

But the most important thing is that the Cuban revolution has maintained the principles of never resorting to torture, of never stooping to crime, without exception to this day, no matter what they say, no matter what they write. We know that a lot of this slander has been written by people in the CIA's pay.

Are there many other examples like it in history? In the world's history there have been many revolutions and in general they were rough, very rough: England's civil wars, the French revolution, the Russian revolution, the Spanish Civil War and the Mexican revolution. We know quite a bit about revolutions and many books have been written about them and about counterrevolutions. Well, one does not even speak of counterrevolutions. Revolutions tend to be generous and counterrevolutions are unfailingly merciless. Just ask the members of the Paris Commune.

In the case of Cuba there has not been one exception. In the whole history of the revolution, there has not been one single case of torture — and I mean that literally — not one political murder, not one disappearance. In our country we do not have the so-called death squads that sprout like mushrooms in this hemisphere's countries. [Audience names several countries] You speak for us! We prefer not to mention names, but everything has happened in our hemisphere.

Why is there no mention made of the United States, where people have been brutally murdered for defending civil rights, men like Martin Luther King and many others. A country where as a rule only Blacks and Hispanics are given the death sentence?

Our country does not have the phenomena we see in others, such as children murdered on the streets allegedly to avoid the spectacle of begging and apparently to fight crime. The revolution eradicated begging, the revolution eliminated gambling, the revolution eliminated drugs, the revolution did away with prostitution.

Yes, unfortunately there can be some cases or tendencies that encourage some *jineteras*, due to economic difficulties and the opening to numerous outside contacts.[6] We do not deny this, and from time to time some may turn up on Fifth Avenue. But one should not confuse decent people with *jineteras*. Such cases exist but we fight against it. We do not tolerate prostitution; we do not legalize prostitution.

There may be some children, encouraged by their parents, who approach tourists and ask them for gum or something else. These are phenomena that we experience due to the special situation that we are living in, at a time of great economic difficulties as the blockade has been strengthened. But these things were not known during the normal times of the revolution.

You won't see people sleeping in doorways covered with newspapers, regardless of our present poverty. There is not a single human being abandoned or without social security, regardless of our present great poverty. The vices we see every day in capitalist societies do not exist in our country. This is an achievement of the revolution.

There is not one child without a school or a teacher; there is not one single citizen who does not receive medical care, starting before birth. Here we start medical care for our citizens when they are still in their mothers' wombs, right from the first weeks after conception.

We are the country in the world with the most doctors per capita, regardless of the special period, and I'm not only referring to the Third World, but to the whole world! More than the Scandinavians, more than the Canadians and all those who are at the top rankings in public health. By reducing infant mortality from 60 to 10 per 1,000 live births and with other pediatric programs, the revolution has saved the lives of more than 300,000 children.[7]

We have the most teachers per capita in the world, regardless of the hardships we suffer. We have the most art teachers per capita in

---

[6] *Jinetera(o)s* refers to women and men who engage in prostitution, usually in tourist areas.

[7] The infant mortality rate refers to the number of infants per 1,000 live births who die before the age of one. Cuba reduced its infant mortality rate from 60 before the revolution to 9.4 today. Since 1973 its infant mortality rate has been the lowest in Latin America and is among the lowest in the world.

the world. We are the country with the most physical education and sports teachers per capita.

That is the country that is being blockaded; that is the country that they are trying to bring to its knees through hunger and disease. Some demand that, in order for them to lift the blockade, we must surrender, we must renounce our political principles, we must renounce socialism and our democratic forms.

Furthermore, quite a confusing document was issued at the Rio conference,[8] despite the noble efforts against it by countries like Brazil, Mexico and others. It was supported by some countries that were very, very hand-in-glove with the United States; I don't want to mention any names. It is a document with a certain degree of confusion that leaves room for erroneous interpretations and some interpret it as supporting the U.S. position of conditioning the blockade's suspension on Cuba making political changes.

Political changes? Is there a country that has made more political changes than we have? What is a revolution, if it's not the most profound and extraordinary of political changes? We made this revolution over 35 years ago, and during those 35 years we have been carrying out political changes, not in search of a formal, alienating democracy that divides people, but rather a democracy that really unites peoples and gives viability to what is most important and essential, which is public participation in fundamental issues. Furthermore, we recently made modifications to the Constitution, based on the principle that the people nominate and the people elect.

I'm not criticizing anybody, but nearly all over the world, including Africa, they are introducing Western political systems, together with neoliberalism and neocolonialism and all those other things. People who have never heard of Voltaire, Danton, Jean-Jacques Rousseau,[9] nor the philosophers of U.S. independence — and

---

[8] The United Nations Conference on Environment and Development (UNCED), also called the World Earth Summit, took place in 1992 in Rio de Janeiro, Brazil.
[9] French philosophers and writers Voltaire (1694–1778) and Jean-Jacques Rousseau (1712–78) epitomized Europe's Age of Enlightenment. Voltaire attacked injustice and intolerance; Rousseau held that people are essentially good but are corrupted by society, necessitating a "social contract." Georges-Jacques Danton (1759–94) was a leader of the French revolution of 1789.

remember that Bolívar[10] in our own hemisphere was very much against the mechanical copying of the European and U.S. systems, which have brought catastrophe, division, subordination and neocolonialism to our countries. We can see societies splitting into thousands of pieces; societies that should be united in their efforts to develop have ended up not only with a multiparty system but with hundreds and even thousands of parties.

Cuba's democracy

We have worked to develop our own system, which we did not copy from anyone. We established the principle that those who nominate in the first instance are the residents. One may or may not agree, but it is as respectable as the Greek democracy that people talk so much about, and without slaves or serfs. Because Greek democracy consisted of just a few that would meet in the plaza — and they had to be few because in those days they did not have microphones — and they would get together to have an election right there. Neither the slaves nor the serfs participated; nor do they today.

When you analyze the electoral results in the United States you discover that they have just elected a new Congress, where undoubtedly there are worrying tendencies toward conservatism and the extreme right; but those are internal matters in the United States. The truth of the matter is, I can assure you, I promise you, we have not made it a condition that the United States renounce its system in order to normalize relations. Just imagine if we told them that they had to have at least 80 percent of the electorate voting. Thirty-eight percent decided to vote and the rest said, "I'm going to the beach," or "I'm going to the movies," or "I'm going home to rest." This is what happened to the "champions" of freedom, human rights and civil rights. It is very much the same in many countries of Latin America. Many people don't even vote. The slaves and the servants say: "What am I going to vote for, if my situation is going to be just the same?"

---

[10] Known as "the Liberator", Simón Bolívar (1783–1830) was a South American revolutionary who led the fight to end Spanish colonialism, beginning in 1819, and was made president of Greater Colombia (now Colombia, Panama, Venezuela and Ecuador). He also helped liberate from Spain both Peru (1824) and Bolivia (1825), which was named in his honor. He is widely seen as a symbol of Latin American unity.

However, 95 percent of Cuban citizens vote in our elections and nobody forces them to vote. Even those who are not with the revolution go and vote, although they may turn in a blank ballot, so as not to vote for this one or for the other, or they vote for one or they vote for the other.

In our nation, I repeat once again, the local residents nominate the candidates and the people elect them. In this way, the possibilities of any citizen being elected are infinitely greater than in any other country.

One good example: I was talking with a Mexican delegation and they said to me: "The youngest of our deputies was here." "How old is he?" They told me: "Twenty-five years old." I was really astounded; but then I suddenly remembered that we have a number of deputies under the age of 20, because the students, from secondary school onwards, take part in the process of selecting candidates, as do all the mass organizations.

The campesinos take part in the process of selecting candidates; the women's organization takes part in the process of selecting candidates; the trade unions take part in the process of selecting candidates; the Committees for the Defense of the revolution take part in the process of selecting candidates. And there are numerous students who are deputies to the National Assembly, and women, campesinos, workers and intellectuals, from all sectors. It is not the party that puts up the candidates. The party does not put up the candidates nor does it elect them. It oversees the elections to make sure that all of the principles and the rules are observed; but it does not take part in any of these electoral processes. That is the situation in our country.

In one of the most recent modifications made in the electoral process, a candidate has to win more than 50 percent of the valid votes to become a deputy.

[Ricardo] Alarcón[11] was explaining some of these things, when he recalled, with a magazine that he had in his hand — he has the advantage of speaking English and he reads a U.S. magazine now and again — how one man had spent $25 million in a campaign to be-

---

[11] Ricardo Alarcón is president of Cuba's National Assembly and its former Foreign Minister and ambassador to the United Nations.

come a member of the U.S. Congress.[12] What kind of democracy is that? How many people have $25 million to spend on a campaign? And in Cuba candidates don't even need to spend $25, although any citizen might have to pay the bus fare to go and vote on the day of the elections.

What kind of democracy is it that requires one to be a millionaire to be able to have all the resources with which to speak and persuade the people to vote for you. And then the candidate does not remember those who voted for him until the next elections four or five years later; he does not think about them ever again; he forgets them.

In our country people can be removed from their posts and the same applies to a municipal delegate as well as the highest official. Anyone can be elected, but they can also be dismissed from those posts. That is our system, which we don't expect all the other countries to apply. It would be absurd to try to make it a model, but it is the system that we have adopted. Nobody imposed it on us; no U.S. governor or supervisor came here to establish an electoral code as they did before.

We drew up the Constitution ourselves, we drew up the electoral code ourselves, we have planned the system ourselves and we have developed it ourselves, which is what you have been defending: the right of a country to establish the regulations, the economic, political and social system that it considers to be appropriate. Anything else in the world is impossible, anything else is absurd, any other aim is insane, and these lunatics go around trying to get everyone to do exactly the same as them, and we don't like their way of doing things.

Cuba's sovereignty cannot be compromised

That is why for us the question of ending the blockade in exchange for political concessions, concessions that correspond to the sovereignty of our country, is unacceptable. It is absolutely unacceptable, it is outrageous, it is exasperating, and really, we would rather perish than give up our sovereignty.

---

[12] Michael Huffington, a right-wing businessman, unsuccessfully ran for the U.S. Senate from California in 1994, spending nearly $25 million in the attempt.

We have had the blockade for many years. However, it is necessary to think about one fact: there was one world when the revolution triumphed; today, 35 years later, there is another world. The world changed and didn't progress, it retrogressed, because the bipolar world wasn't to anyone's liking, but the unipolar world is much less to our liking.

When the revolution triumphed, there was a bipolar world. The United States imposed the blockade on us from almost the first moments. It began by doing away with the sugar markets and it cut off our supply of fuel. Imagine the new revolution in those circumstances! Of course they cut off our supply of machinery, of spare parts, of everything, but there was the Soviet Union and the socialist bloc.

That was lucky for us, because faced with the U.S. blockade, 90 miles away, there was another power in the world, another movement in the world which had a revolutionary origin, and which was at odds with U.S. imperialism. Thanks to that movement we could find markets for our sugar, supplies of oil, raw materials, food, many things. That was explained here.

We were paid preferential prices; however, it is necessary to say that not only Cuba was paid preferential prices. The Lomé Convention[13] established preferential prices for sugar and other products for many countries that were ex-colonies. In the United States itself, when it was a major sugar market, there were also preferential prices, before they snatched away our quota and redistributed it throughout Latin America and other parts of the world. As Lage[14] explained, 80 percent of the sugar in the world is traded through preferential prices. And very much in accordance with the principles of their political doctrine, the socialist countries paid us preferential prices.

That was the policy which we defended for all of the countries of the Third World, because it was the only way of reducing the great difference that existed between the developed countries and the

---

[13] The Lomé Convention of 1974 regulated economic relations between African, Caribbean and Pacific nations and the European Economic Community. It was created by the Organization of African Unity (OAU) in response to a call from the United Nations for a new international economic order.

[14] Carlos Lage Dávila is vice-president of the Council of State and secretary of the Executive Committee of the Council of Ministers.

underdeveloped countries. It was a demand of the world, it was a demand of all the countries of the Third World. It was mutually advantageous, because although they paid us preferential prices, it cost more to produce sugar in the Soviet Union than the prices they paid us for sugar. But at any rate, we benefited from those preferential prices, and we used the money to purchase fuel, raw materials and many things.

Collapse of the Soviet Union

In our situation it so happened that the Soviet Union and the socialist bloc collapsed and the blockade was tightened. As long as the socialist bloc and the Soviet Union existed we managed better, we could endure the difficulties. Our economy even grew under those conditions throughout nearly 30 years and attained an extraordinary social development.

However, it was in that world that the Cuban revolution was born. There were no other alternatives in the midst of the country being blockaded by the most powerful country in the world. That is why the disappearance of the socialist bloc and the Soviet Union was such a terrible blow for us, given that the existing blockade was not only maintained but was also strengthened. For that reason our country lost 70 percent of our imports, and I wonder if any other country in the world would have been able to withstand a similar blow, and I wonder how many days they would have been able to withstand it — a week, two weeks or a month. How would we have been able to if it hadn't been for the people's support for the revolution? How would we be able to withstand it, really, without our political system, without our democratic system, without the people's direct participation in all of the fundamental issues, which is true democracy?

Would any other Latin American country have been able to withstand an abrupt 70 percent drop in imports? Would any European country have been able to endure a similar trial? The politicians would have abandoned their principles and capitulated in an instant; but we have dignity, we have a sense of honor and we stick to our principles. For us these principles are worth more than life itself and we have never sold out our principles, never!

When we helped the Central American revolutionaries, the United States said that they would remove the blockade if we stopped helping them, and nothing of the kind ever crossed our minds. On other occasions they said that they would be prepared to remove the blockade if we stopped helping Angola and other African countries, and the idea of selling out our relations with other countries never crossed our minds. On other occasions, they said they would remove the blockade if we broke off our links with the Soviet Union, and it never occurred to us to do anything of the kind, because we are not a party or a political leadership that sells out its principles. The blockade will never end at that price, because it is a price that we are not prepared to pay.

That situation led us to the special period.

We had been working on some excellent programs before the socialist catastrophe, excellent programs in all fields. We were carrying out a process of rectification of errors and negative tendencies, of old errors and new errors, of old tendencies and new tendencies. And we were working very intensely when that debacle led us into what we could call a double blockade, because as soon as the breakup of the socialist bloc and the breakup of the Soviet Union occurred, and even before the breakup of the Soviet Union, the United States was strongly pressuring those countries to stop trading with Cuba. And when the Soviet Union finally disintegrated, the United States put on extreme pressure, and not without success, to cut off trade and economic relations between the countries of the old socialist bloc, the Soviet Union and Cuba.

So our country found itself enveloped in a double blockade. Nevertheless, we had to save the nation, we had to save the revolution and we had to save socialism. We talk about saving the gains of socialism, because we can't say at this time that we are building socialism, but rather that we are defending what we have done, we are defending our achievements.

This is a fundamental objective in a world that has changed in such a radical way, in which all the power of the United States has been turned against us. They don't impose conditions on China, a huge country, an immense country, which defends the ideas of socialism. They don't impose conditions on Vietnam, a marvelous and heroic country. Today there is no blockade against them, but there is a blockade against us. Put yourselves in the place of our party and our government. And in these such difficult conditions that have never existed before, we must save the nation, save the revolution and save the achievements of socialism.

What measures would it be necessary to take in this world which exists today and which, of course, won't always exist? Those are illusions held by those who believe that neoliberalism is already the *ne plus ultra*, that it is the be-all and end-all for capitalism; these are illusions that they have. The world will teach us many lessons.

The globalization of poverty

Now they talk about the globalization of the economy. We'll see what is left from this globalization for the countries of the Third World, with the disappearance of all the current defense mechanisms of the Third World, which must compete with the technology and the immense development of the industrialized capitalist countries. Now the industrialized countries will try more than ever to exploit the natural resources and the cheap work force of the Third World, to accumulate more and more capital. However, it is superdeveloped capitalism, as in Europe, for example, that has more unemployed people all the time; and the more development, the more unemployed there are. What will happen with our countries? There will be a globalization of the differences, of the social injustice, the globalization of poverty.

However, this is the world we face, with which we must trade and exchange our products, in which we have to survive. That is why we must adapt to that world and adopt those measures which we consider essential, with a very clear objective.

This is not to say that everything that we are doing is solely the result of the new situation. We have made changes as we go along, and even the idea of introducing foreign capital came up before the special period. We had realized that specific areas could not be developed because there wasn't the capital or the technology to do so, because the socialist countries didn't have them. However, we have had to open up more; we have had to create what we could call a pretty large opening to foreign investment. That was explained here: in Cuba's circumstances today, without capital, without technology and without markets, we couldn't develop.[15] Hence, all of the measures, changes and reforms that we have been making, in one way and another, have the objective, as was stated in this conference, of safeguarding our independence and the revolution along with the achievements of socialism, which is to say, to preserve socialism or the right to continue constructing socialism when circumstances allow it.

We are making changes, but without giving up our independence and sovereignty. We are making changes, but without giving up the real principle of a government of the people, by the people and for the people; which, translated into revolutionary language, is the government of the workers, by the workers and for the workers. It's not a government of the bourgeoisie, by the bourgeoisie and for the bourgeoisie; nor a government of the capitalists, by the capitalists and for the capitalists; nor a government of the transnationals, by the transnationals and for the transnationals; nor a government of the imperialists, by the imperialists and for the imperialists.

That is the big difference, whatever changes and reforms we carry out. If some day we renounced all this we would be renouncing the lifeblood of the revolution.

Cuba's solidarity with the world

We have shown solidarity with the world, although it's not our task now to talk about this solidarity. As far as our solidarity is concerned, we should do the most and talk the least, because we're not going to make any apology for our conduct.

A few minutes ago, before starting the final part of this event, a comrade said: "Look at how many things Cuba has done. When visitors from one country or another talk, when they talk about doctors, students, people that were trained here, in one activity or another, it is clear that in these years our country has carried out many things." For us, solidarity and internationalism are a matter of principle, and a sacred one at that.

To provide an example, I'm going to give a few statistics. More than 15,000 Cuban doctors have given free services in dozens of

---

[15] Beginning in 1992, Cuba made a series of economic reforms, including permitting foreign investment in Cuba, decriminalizing the possession of U.S. dollars, vastly expanding tourism and creating certain forms of taxation.

countries in these years of the revolution; more than 15,000 doctors have fulfilled internationalist missions as doctors.

Suffice it to say that at one point we had three times more doctors working for free in the Third World than did the World Health Organization; and we didn't have a lot of resources either, only minimum resources. We only had the honor of our health workers, with their internationalist calling. How many lives have they saved? And I wonder, is it fair to blockade a country that has done this?

More than 26,000 Cuban teachers have served abroad. How many hundreds of thousands of children have we educated with our teachers in foreign countries? And we haven't only sent primary and secondary schoolteachers, but university professors. We have founded medical schools in diverse countries of the world. Is it fair to blockade a country that has done all this, and still does it to a certain degree?

Half a million Cubans have completed internationalist missions of different types, half a million Cubans! I ask if any other small country, and even medium or big countries, has had this record.

The Africans have been very generous, very noble, and have wanted to recall here Cuba's solidarity and aid in the war against colonialism, the war against foreign aggression, the war against apartheid and racism.

As I said here, our soldiers were fighting in southern Angola — 40,000 men! They were fighting alongside the Angolan troops, who acted and fought heroically. There were Cubans in southern Angola facing up to the South Africans after the battle of Cuito Cuanavale,[16] and when our counteroffensive was launched in southwest Angola these men and women were exposed to the possibility of nuclear warfare. We knew it, and the distribution of forces in that offensive took into account the possibility that the enemy could use nuclear weapons.

At one point we had 25,000 foreign students in our universities. Cuba was the country with more scholarships per capita than any-

---

[16] On March 23, 1988, South African forces, in their fifth major offensive against Cuito Cuanavale in southern Angola, were decisively defeated with the help of Cuban troops. Cubans call the battle the African Battle of Playa Girón (Bay of Pigs). Cuba's role in Southern Africa changed the course of negotiations between Angola and South Africa and contributed to the independence of Namibia.

where else in the world, and we didn't brag about it. We just went on our way, fulfilling the task of education as [José] Martí taught us, and we did what we could for other countries.

I think that this extraordinary conference, your noble and generous words and words of solidarity, reflect in part the history of our own revolution's solidarity. This has greatly encouraged us and gives us the strength to keep going.

There are a lot of choices in this day and age: the choice of freedom, the choice of sovereignty, the choice of independence, and the choice of social justice. Social justice is acquiring such force as an idea — in the midst of neoliberalism, which is the negation of every principle of justice — that even some international agencies talk about it. The Inter-American Development Bank talks more and more about the need for social justice in this hemisphere. Even the World Bank is talking about social justice! They are the champions of neoliberalism and they talk about social justice, because they realize that the differences are so great and are still growing, and they would like to make the dream of neoliberalism come true, of capitalism with social justice. They are afraid that misery, hunger and poverty will undermine the bases of the neoliberalism that they praise so much, and that is why they talk about social justice.

But we know that only the people can achieve social justice and that neoliberalism and social justice are incompatible, they are irreconcilable; that a superdeveloped world next to an underdeveloped world is incompatible, irreconcilable. We know that the former will get richer and richer, while the latter will get poorer and poorer, and this is an irrefutable reality.

Your presence here shows that just ideas live on, that noble ideas live on, that values live on. And we have to multiply these ideas and values just as Jesus Christ multiplied the loaves and fishes.

The church talks about giving opportunities to the poor, and this seems excellent to us, but I think that today's world needs more than choices: it needs energetic, tenacious and consistent struggle by the poor themselves. I should have said "churches" instead of "the church," considering that we're not only talking about the Catholic church.

We must wage an unending battle against the causes of poverty, an inexorable offensive against capitalism, against neoliberalism, against imperialism, until the day when we can no longer speak of billions of human beings who are hungry, who don't have schools, hospitals, a roof over their head, or even the most elemental means of living.

This planet is getting close to having six billion inhabitants; in one century the population has increased fourfold. The threats that humanity suffers today are multiple; not only social, but economic, political and military.

Someone here was saying — I think it was Robertico [Robaina][17] — that nowadays they call wars "humanitarian missions" or "peace operations." Wars threaten us from all sides, interventions threaten us from all sides. But the world is also being threatened by destruction of the natural conditions for life, the destruction of the environment, a problem which is getting more and more attention and increasingly moves the conscience of humanity. We will have to make a huge effort in every sense of the word to save humanity from all these risks.

And what is the historical origin of this situation? Could anyone deny that it was colonialism, neocolonialism and imperialism? Could anyone deny that it was capitalism? We are very conscious of all this, despite the setbacks suffered by the progressive movement, the revolutionary movement and the socialist movement.

But we'll say it here and now, dear friends. We will never return to capitalism! Not to savage capitalism — or as Pérez Esquivel likes to call it, cannibal capitalism — or to moderate capitalism, if this exists. We don't want to go back, and we won't go back!

We know what our duties and obligations are. We've withstood almost five hard years already, when others thought the Cuban revolution would quickly disappear off the face of the earth.

We're working persistently and harder all the time, and even putting more and more emphasis on the subjective, on our own errors, our own deficiencies; emphasizing the subjective so that the objective does not become a pretext for deficiencies.

We've still got to raise the consciousness of our people. We still have to explain why we need to reduce the excess currency in circulation and the methods used to continue gathering up the excess

---

[17] Roberto Robaina is Cuba's Foreign Minister. He was previously first secretary of the Young Communist Union (UJC).

without using shock therapy. We have to look for efficiency in agriculture and industry.[18]

I know that the issue of food production has been a worry of yours, expressed here. I must say that we are forced to produce food without fertilizers, without pesticides, without weedkillers, often without fuel, resorting to animal traction, faced with the need to feed the 80 percent of the population living in urban zones. Cuba, unlike Vietnam or China, has only 20 percent of the population in the countryside and 80 percent in the cities. They have the inverse, 75 percent to 80 percent in the countryside and 20 percent to 25 percent in the cities.

We even have a labor shortage in rural areas. Our agriculture and sugar industry had been mechanized, like many other sectors of the economy. Someone asked whether we should produce sugar or not. We don't have any other choice than to produce sugar; we have to produce it. Now, it has become more expensive for the sugar mills and machines to produce less because of a lack of fertilizer and irrigation, for example. In general, we know how to produce food, but we've had to deal with a great scarcity of supplies for food production.

We've had to develop other areas. Tourism has already been mentioned here. It has become a necessity, although it wasn't promoted in the first years of the revolution because it has its good side and its bad side. And since we can't live with the hope of being in an ivory tower, we have to get mixed up with the problems of this world. And, based on the idea that virtue is born of the struggle against vice, just as magnificent flowers bloom from cow dung, we have to get used to living with all these types of problems. We have to look for resources in convertible currency to make these supplies available. The livestock has been left without feed, without irrigated land, without fuel.

---

[18] Shortages resulting from the blockade have made many jobs superfluous as factories have been forced to close. Since Cuban workers had continued to receive their wages, in the absence of goods to purchase the supply of cash became excessive, leading to high inflation and an unstable peso. During the special period, Cuba has implemented a series of economic measures to balance the country's internal finances, including taxation and charging fees for previously free services, such as sports and cultural events. The economic reform policies put into effect in recent years have been stabilizing the peso and the economy.

The problems we've had to deal with are not easy, but we're handling it, accomplishing what Robertico said about sharing the little we have among many, rather than a lot among a few. We've been sharing what we have.

And then, under these incredibly difficult conditions — I repeat, there is not a single school without a teacher, not a child without a school, not a patient without a doctor or hospital — we maintain social security, we maintain our cultural development, the development of sports. We even came in fifth place in the [1992] Olympic Games in the midst of the special period. This gives you an idea of our strength in exceptionally difficult conditions.

Therefore, when we share the little we have among everyone, a lot of things can be done, and there are many countries in the world that have much more than we do and do very few things.

This event concludes, really, as an unforgettable lesson for all of us, and we hope for a lot, we hope for so much from this battle that you propose to fight shoulder to shoulder with us to end the blockade, to end the hostility against our country, to defend hope. Not because we have been predestined to be anyone's hope. We don't consider ourselves a people bound by destiny. We constitute a small people, a modest people, to whom history has in these particular circumstances assigned the role of what we're defending: our most sacred ideals, our most sacred rights. You all see this as hope.

We understand what it would mean for all the progressive forces, for all the revolutionary forces, for all lovers of peace and justice in the world if the United States succeeded in crushing the Cuban revolution. And because of this we consider defending the revolution along with you to be our most sacred duty, even at the cost of death.

Thank you, thank you very much, a million times thank you.

Reflections on the Cuban revolution

Speech of July 26, 1995

President Fidel Castro commemorates the attack on the Moncada Garrison, the opening battle of the Cuban revolution, at the ceremony marking its 42nd anniversary on July 26, 1995, at Guantánamo's Mariana Grajales Revolution Square.

It gives me much pleasure to be with you on the 42nd anniversary of the attack on the Moncada Garrison.[1] Guantánamo received the honor of being the site of this anniversary event not only in recognition of its outstanding work on many fronts, but especially because of the dignified and efficient manner in which its people confronted the series of natural disasters that affected this province.

By chance we are also celebrating in Guantánamo the centenary anniversary of Martí's and Gómez's landing in Playitas, and that of Maceo with Crombet and other patriots in Duaba.[2] This year we have also commemorated the centennial of José Martí's death in combat in Dos Ríos.

---

[1] On July 26, 1953, Fidel and a small group of revolutionaries attacked the Moncada Garrison in Santiago de Cuba. At least 70 of the revolutionaries were killed and the rest imprisoned, including Fidel. From that battle emerged the July 26 Movement whose goals became known as the Moncada Program.

[2] José Martí, Maximo Gómez, Antonio Maceo and Flor Crombet were leaders of the First War for Cuba's Independence from Spain, the Ten Years' War, from October 1868 to May 1878.

This moment evokes many emotions and memories. However, the principal one to bear in mind is that our struggle for independence was initiated 127 years ago; that is to say, our battles for sovereignty, liberty, justice and the dignity of our small but patriotic and heroic nation. Cuba lies at the very gates of a powerful and expansionist nation which has never ceased to extend its frontiers. This was first at the expense of the indigenous peoples, who occupied a great part of the current territory of the United States and who were virtually exterminated, and then at the expense of the peoples of Latin America and the Caribbean. Few countries in the world have had to face a more colossal challenge and risk than that met by Cuba, the ripe apple that by its own weight would have to fall into the hands of the growing empire.

Even then there were people who thought that the task was an impossible one, but there were also others who have never resigned themselves to the idea of renouncing their independence, their culture and their national identity. Thanks to those outstanding precursors, today we are speaking in Spanish here, and not in English.

The efforts and sacrifices of entire generations of Cubans did not succeed in realizing their revolutionary dreams of justice and full independence. However, they sowed the seeds and prepared the ground. We could not continue being a foreign power's colony; we could not continue to be obedient servants of the United States. We could not continue to be a country of landless campesinos, of children without schools, of sick people without doctors. A country of exploited workers, of Blacks without rights, women who faced discrimination, young people without any future, a work force without employment, of humiliated citizens. A country whose laws were daily mocked, where corruption was rampant, and whose national anthem and flag lacked any meaning. Forced evictions, abhorrent crimes — this was the caricature of a republic that the U.S. intervention made of our nation.

Any person plundering public funds, corrupt politicians or those responsible for atrocious crimes of repression had a safe haven in the United States, especially if they acted in the name of that country's economic interests or anticommunist ideology.

All this occurred and has continued to occur in recent years in numerous countries in our hemisphere. Who initiated the Latin

American repressive forces into crime, torture, mass disappearances, death squads, clandestine cemeteries and other abhorrent practices?

The revolution is launched

The July 26 armed uprising in 1953 was carried out against everything that happened in Cuba under Batista,[3] that consummate servant of U.S. interests and reactionary ideology. The revolution, which was launched with the attack on the Moncada and was continued in prison, and the *Granma* landing,[4] the Sierra Maestra, the underground struggles, in the cities, mountains and plains, led us to the victory of January 1, 1959. We were in charge of our own future for the first time in history.

The Moncada program was rigorously fulfilled within a relatively short space of time. Secular privileges and inequalities were swept away. It was not a socialist program, but it contained the basic elements for future advances in that direction. If we, the principal leaders, had socialist ideas and convictions, or more precisely, Marxist-Leninist ideas, as we have said many times, the Cuban revolution was not as yet a socialist one.

However, this process was rapidly accelerated as a consequence of the aggressive policy adopted by the U.S. government. The first Agrarian Reform Law[5] had barely been approved in May 1959 when

---

[3] Fulgencio Batista was a military officer in the Cuban army who led the "Sergeants' Revolt" in September 1933, after which he held power as a "strongman," controlling the presidency from behind the scenes with U.S. support, until 1940. By manipulating the 1940 elections, he was elected president, a post he held until 1944, when Ramón Grau San Martín was elected president. In 1952, Batista carried out a coup, suspending the Constitution and becoming Cuba's dictator. The revolution, led by Fidel Castro, overthrew Batista's corrupt, authoritarian regime on New Year's Day, 1959.

[4] After being released from prison, on May 15, 1955, along with the other revolutionaries captured in 1953, Fidel went into exile in Mexico and began to prepare an expedition to return to Cuba to launch the revolution. On December 2, 1956, Fidel, with his brother Raúl Castro, Che Guevara and 79 other revolutionaries, landed in Oriente Province on the *Granma* cabin cruiser. Though most were killed, the survivors established a base of operations in the Sierra Maestra mountains, joined by revolutionaries who had been organizing inside Cuba.

[5] The first Agrarian Reform Law, signed by Fidel on May 17, 1959, put a limit on land holdings and expropriated the remainder with compensation to the owners, with the land to be distributed to landless Cubans. At the time, foreign-

that country's administration decided to liquidate the revolution by employing mercenary forces in a similar style to that used against the government of Jacobo Arbenz in Guatemala in 1954, when he also decided to carry out an agrarian reform. Prior to this point, the U.S. government had applied heavy economic aggression against our country. Via a process of U.S. government measures and Cuban responses, within a brief period of time the majority of U.S. companies in Cuba were nationalized. These measures were followed by the nationalization of the principal private Cuban companies, whose proprietors, as a general rule, made common cause with U.S. policy.

In this way, the day after the treacherous bombing of our air bases, on April 16, 1961, the eve of the Bay of Pigs invasion, [6] in front of tens of thousands of armed militia members, the socialist character of the revolution was proclaimed. In the Sierra Maestra we fought for the Moncada program; in the Bay of Pigs battle our heroic people shed their blood for socialism, in full view of a powerful U.S. naval squadron a few miles off our coasts, ready to intervene.

The historic circumstances in which our struggle took place demonstrate that it could not be described as revolutionary if it had not been an anti-imperialist and, moreover, socialist struggle. Only socialism was able to so closely unite the great popular masses to carry out the great moral, political, economic and social battle which lay ahead of us, as well as preparing us to act in the military terrain if the country was invaded. It was essential to win total justice, as Martí said to Juan Gualberto Gómez.[7] Only socialism as a political, economic and social regime could provide total justice.

---

ers owned 75 percent of arable land, with five U.S. sugar companies owning or controlling more than two million acres. The new law limited privately owned sugarcane land to 3,300 acres per owner.

[6] The U.S. prepared for the Bay of Pigs invasion by bombing Cuban defenses on April 15, 1961, killing seven Cubans. The CIA tried to make the attack look as if it had been carried out by counterrevolutionary Cubans, but the ruse was quickly uncovered. The next day, April 16, then-Prime Minister Fidel Castro announced for the first time the socialist character of the revolution. The U.S.-backed mercenary forces invaded on April 17 and were defeated on April 19.

[7] Juan Gualberto Gómez, a mulatto Cuban, was sent to France as a youth to learn a trade. While there he organized support for the Ten Years' War (1868–78). He later returned to Cuba and became a close associate of José Martí. After the Cuban Revolutionary Party was formed in 1892, Gualberto Gómez was

The world in which this long struggle has been waged for over 36 years — this is not the moment to detail its extraordinary history — was not designed by us; it was already shaped on January 1, 1959. But nobody should have the slightest doubt that whether the Soviet Union and the socialist bloc had existed or not, we would have attacked the Moncada Garrison, we would have landed in the *Granma*, we would have achieved the January 1 revolution, and we would have fought at the Bay of Pigs.

When Maceo led the Baraguá protest,[8] when Martí landed in Playitas, when the *mambí* independence fighters[9] carried out their glorious westward march, when Cuba fought alone against 300,000 Spanish soldiers, the Soviet Union and the socialist camp did not exist. We didn't even have any contact or relations with those countries; that only occurred after our victory.

The historical coincidence of the emergence of the Cuban revolution and the existence of the Soviet Union and the socialist camp was a chance event, albeit an extraordinarily useful one, when our little country was mercilessly blockaded in the economic field and militarily harassed and threatened by the United States.

For anyone who still harbors the slightest doubt over what I have just said, one undeniable fact is sufficient. When the socialist camp and the Soviet Union disappeared, our people, in spite of abruptly losing 70 percent of their imported goods and all military

---

appointed the party's main representative in Cuba. He helped lay the groundwork for the revolutionary forces in exile before the 1895 War of Independence. Through letters he was in constant communication with Martí, who lived in New York City.

[8] On October 10, 1868, Cuba's First War of Independence, the Ten Years' War, began when plantation owner Carlos Manuel de Céspedes led 37 other owners in proclaiming Cuba's independence from Spain. Céspedes freed and armed his slaves. In February 1878, Spanish General Arsenio Martínez Campos offered a peace agreement which was accepted by the House of Representatives of the Republic of Cuba in Arms; this agreement, called the Zanjón Treaty, was then signed with Spain. Cuban General Antonio Maceo and other leaders, however, opposed the agreement because it did not provide independence for Cuba or abolish slavery. On March 15, General Maceo met with General Martínez at Mangos de Baraguá and presented the Protest of Baraguá. Fighting resumed shortly after, but the Cuban troops were forced to surrender in May 1878.

[9] The *mambises* were the Cuban independence fighters during the First War of Independence.

cooperation, didn't hesitate for a second, but went ahead to defend, at all cost, their independence, their exceptional social conquests, their glorious history, their ideals, their revolution and the fruit of the blood shed by their children within and outside Cuba.

Many people who were incapable of perceiving the courage of this people believed that the revolution would collapse in a matter of days or weeks, and here we are not only resisting, but little by little once more beginning to gain ground.

The special period
Compatriots: Let us not forget, even for a second, the effort and sacrifice the special period has signified for our people. It is also very difficult for the revolution to continue to wage the struggle while having to daily attend to the problems and needs of 11 million people. How to ensure that no child goes without milk, that the sick do not lack the medical care they need, that there are minimum levels of food, electricity, water, domestic fuel, transportation and the many other products and services required by the population!

Dealing with the problems of a guerrilla army in the mountains is not the same as attending to the needs of an entire nation while huge efforts are being made by our enemies to maintain the blockade and place obstacles in the way of everything. What we are doing today has never been in vain, nor will it ever be. It is a historically unprecedented feat that not one single school, hospital, senior citizens' home or children's day-care center has been closed.

The infant mortality rate is now lower than at the beginning of the special period, and there are many more doctors; the country's security and defense capacities have been strengthened; advances have been made in scientific research, and in the cultural and sports fields; our agricultural and industrial sectors are functioning; orderly work is going ahead in all areas and some of the fruits of this are already becoming apparent. Oil, nickel, electricity, steel and cement production are on the increase, as well as root and garden vegetables and other items. The gross domestic product saw a 2 percent increase in the first six months of 1995, a modest figure, but worth noting. It would have been higher without decreased production in the sugarcane industry, where special efforts are now being made which cannot fail to produce positive results in the near future.

Within the space of less than a year, the excess of liquid cash circulation among the population was reduced by almost 2.7 billion pesos. The peso is regaining value: one year ago, the street exchange value was over 130 pesos to the dollar; today it stands at barely 35.[10] So progress is being made in organizing the country's internal finances. But this requires an increasingly strict fulfillment of the policy that has been outlined, which as yet has not been fully implemented, and at no time should we fall into the temptation of putting new pesos into circulation. As the excess of surplus cash in circulation diminishes, the task of further reducing it becomes more difficult, although this is still essential. The benefits can be seen in an increased interest in work and the greater need to earn a wage.

Tax collection must be carried out more rigorously.

However, the lack of hard currency to pay for required imports constitutes a serious problem for our economy. This is the principal obstacle confronting us today. Some financing is being made available at elevated costs. On occasion, a price increase in one single item, such as fuel, foodstuffs or powdered milk, leads to a considerable deficit. This is a reality to take into account.

Recently, a series of measures have been implemented, in line with a set of changes and points of view within the economic sphere.

Economic reforms not a return to capitalism
Some of these measures are wide-reaching and radical, with a view to improving the work being carried out in this sphere, particularly in order to adapt our economy to the realities of today's world. Other countries such as China and Vietnam have been doing this for some time, but does this maybe signify the renunciation of our socialist ideals and our Marxist-Leninist convictions? Quite the contrary.

As true Marxist-Leninists we have to take this course of action, with all the courage and realism demanded by the circumstances. However, this does not imply, as some people seem to think, a return to capitalism, and much less a crazy and unchecked rush in that direction. The incredible disasters that have taken place in the countries of the former Soviet Union, in spite of its vast resources in energy and raw materials as well as foreign aid, in contrast to the

---

[10] The reforms continue to increase the value of the peso. As of March 1996, the unofficial exchange rate was 25 pesos to the dollar.

impressive successes in China and Vietnam, are a clear indication of what should and should not be done if we wish to save the revolution and socialism. This is discounting the fact that none of those countries are being blockaded by the United States. Cuba, on the other hand, is blockaded to the hilt, with rage and fury. The whole economic arsenal of the hegemonic empire is currently focused on us. For this reason only our socialism, our serenity and the level-headedness with which we have tackled our problems have made the miracle of our resistance possible.

The unquestionable capitalist elements introduced into our country have been accompanied by the damaging and alienating effects of that system. The phenomenon of bribery and corruption, unheard of during the 30 years of trade with the Soviet Union, can be appreciated in an incipient and growing form in our economic relations with capitalism. It should be said, in all fairness, that we have relations with many responsible capitalists, who behave in an appropriate manner; others are using the universal capitalist practices of bribery and corruption, in a discreet or blatant manner.

There are also people who have let themselves be carried away by an avidity for hard currency, to the point of selling their souls. Large-scale tourism, the decriminalization of the possession of hard currency, the institutions trading in that currency, measures which were unavoidable, have their inevitable cost.

The style and behavior of some people reveal the pleasure they take in the entrepreneurial role. Others want to set up their own enterprises or small businesses at any cost to operate in hard currency in their work centers or institutions, more often than not with a view to misspending it, violating the carefully established norms in this area. The party and the government will have to wage a colossal battle against such tendencies before they develop into a cancer devouring our ethics and revolutionary spirit. We have to take an inexorable stance against those persons who violate our most sacred principles. The blood of so many Cubans was not shed to let in such shameful conduct at the nation's most critical moment.

The "two-track" attack of the United States

The battle we have to fight is a hard one, but the firm determination in our souls must be harder. The enemy's undertaking to destroy us is without respite. There are two strategies: one coming from the extreme right elements in U.S. politics who dream of strangling us with an even tighter blockade, if that were possible, and of sweeping us off the face of the earth by whatever means necessary. They are the ones who promote legislation such as the Helms-Burton bill,[11] well-known by our people who have examined it closely, and other draconian measures. They are the ones who would like to destroy us from outside.

The other strategy is championed by those who want to penetrate our nation, to weaken us, to create all kinds of counterrevolutionary organizations and to destabilize the country regardless of the consequences. They have developed a whole theory and a program designed to this end. These persons want to exert their influence through wide-ranging exchanges with diverse sectors they believe they can influence, by granting generous scholarships, by dazzling us with their million-dollar institutions, their technology, their social research centers. They do not allow U.S. citizens to travel to Cuba, to get to know the island and to have a holiday here, but they are prepared to send sociologists, philosophers, historians, Cuba specialists, English professors and other academics to our universities to "enlighten" us. These people yes, but the last thing in the world they will do is to send professors of cybernetics, computer science or spheres of technology which have no relation to ideology and who could be of some use to the country. That is to say, the so-called track two of the Torricelli Act.[12] Those are the ones who would like to destroy us from within.

---

[11] The Helms-Burton bill, approved in the U.S. House of Representatives in September 1995, further strengthens the U.S. blockade against Cuba. It punishes countries and individuals that do business with Cuba and allows U.S. corporations and individuals that claim their property was expropriated by the revolution to sue companies or individuals now operating on that property in U.S. courts. The bill was signed into law by President Clinton in March 1996.

[12] The Torricelli Act, officially the Cuban Democracy Act of 1992, was signed into law in October 1992 by President George Bush. In addition to severe economic restrictions on and sanctions against companies and countries that do business with Cuba, it contains provisions to try to undermine Cuban society by strengthening U.S. telecommunications with Cuba, funding anticommunist propaganda and encouraging right-wing and anti-government groups to infiltrate the island.

There are many courageous and noble U.S. citizens in all spheres, businesspeople included, who are not involved in either of these two strategies.

Meanwhile, within U.S. territory — and this is very serious — and without any attempt at discretion, acts of terrorism against the Cuban population and in vital areas of the economy are being actively planned and set in operation, including, once again, frenetically planned attempts on the lives of the revolution's leaders. The main center for such activities is the so-called Cuban American National Foundation.[13] It is absolutely inconceivable that the CIA and FBI are not aware of such plans, given that presumably they have infiltrated those organizations, many of whose members have had relations with them.

Now that our country has been opened up to tourism and there is a possibility of travel between Cuba and the United States, the execution of such plans is facilitated, and the introduction of a variety of channels to achieve such ends makes them more feasible.

Our security corps is on the alert in the context of such activities, and is working to prevent their occurrence.

These words are not spoken without proof. We are giving a timely warning and hope that no one will later regret the rigor with which the revolutionary laws sanction these crimes, nor try to appeal to the revolution's generosity.

To this can be added the emission of more than one thousand hours per week of radio broadcasts inciting sabotage, actions against the economy and the assassination of political leaders.

It is absolutely shameful that, in the wake of the brutal crime that took place in Oklahoma, acts of terrorism against Cuba are being organized and put into action from the United States.

What I have said up to this point gives you some idea of how arduous our struggle is and will be. You should also take into account that the United States is in its electoral process and the extreme right elements, which now have majority control in Congress,

---

[13] The Cuban American National Foundation (CANF), one of the most right-wing anticommunist Cuban exile organizations, was founded in 1981 by wealthy Cuban exiles in Miami. Funded by the CIA, its purpose is to oppose and overthrow the Cuban government. Chair Jorge Mas Canosa has worked in close collaboration with the U.S. government.

are aspiring not only to erase the social measures dating back to the Roosevelt era, but also to form the next U.S. government, with all the consequences this could have for the world as a whole.

Blockade requires superhuman effort

Compatriots: We have to be prepared for all these possibilities. The blockade conditions under which we are obliged to resist and advance demand a superhuman effort, an immutable steadfastness and absolute integrity on the part of everyone.

In normal times, when resources were fully available and during a period of substantial egalitarianism, many people grew accustomed to receiving everything and contributing very little. A critical analysis will remind us of inflated rosters in the areas of production and services, absenteeism under any pretext, the four or five hours' working day in several agricultural enterprises, the excess expenditure in fuel and raw materials, and the misuse of agricultural machinery and transportation. We cannot permit any of these luxuries today.

In the recent period, great effort has gone into demanding much more of the party and state cadres. There have been widespread replacements, and a great commitment has been shown by everyone. However, we can still observe errors, weaknesses, irresponsibility, and incompetence.

As at no other time in our history, today we demand of our workers and our cadres the maximum of patriotism, moral values and dignity. Alongside cases and examples that are disheartening are a growing number of men and women who demonstrate a behavior worthy of the times in which we live. A rebirth of revolutionary spirit is apparent throughout the country. It is moving to observe men and women working in the fields or factories in tennis shoes or even barefoot. This should serve as an example to all those who are comfortably off or who do not have enough confidence in the virtues of their people.

Our compatriots' exceptional humanity and political qualities were made evident during our latest elections, a clear message to the world of what Cuba is and a solid confirmation of how a people with a high cultural level and a solid political awareness acted. Our enemies had constructed grand illusions of seeing the revolution weakened and debilitated by the harsh realities of the special period.

Cuba's recent elections a moral victory

These elections were so distinctive in terms of what happens almost everywhere else! And so distinct from what happens in the United States! Even though the option to vote or not is absolutely open, there was a turnout of 97.1 percent. Even assuming there was not one single voting error and that no blank ballot was the result of disagreement with the choice of candidate and that both were expressions of discontent or opposition, void or spoiled ballots totaled only 11.2 percent, barely 0.6 percent more than in 1992. Clearly, a visible deterioration or a relative manifestation of discouragement was to be expected, given the harsh conditions which have befallen our thousand times heroic people, but this did not happen. Another Bay of Pigs moral victory over those who are trying to bring us to our knees!

People of Guantánamo: I have said very little about you, and as I don't want to talk too extensively, I have to be brief. The statistics reflecting Guantánamo province's work would be interminable. I am going to give no more than two examples, just to offer the United States an example of social development. Guantánamo, Cuba's poorest province, with a doctor for every 271 inhabitants, has more doctors per capita than the United States, and with an infant mortality rate of 9.2 percent, it has less infant mortality than that country's capital.

I warmly congratulate you for having gained the position of being the site of the main celebrations for July 26.[14]

To the women of Cuba, to whom this commemoration is dedicated, to speak of you I would have to begin this speech again. I just wonder if there is any part of the world where 62 percent of the technical work force is made up of women, and if what we have achieved up until now would have been possible without you. I congratulate you equally for the selflessness and sacrifice which have made you worthy of this just honor!

---

[14] Each year one of Cuba's 14 provinces is selected to host the main July 26 celebration, based on exceptional production and other social accomplishments of the year.

Soldiers of the heroic Border Brigade, I congratulate you for having received the Major General José Maceo[15] combat glory flag! You have written an indelible page of courage in the history of the revolution and have given a supreme example of generosity in the face of danger and in saving the lives of people who had renounced their nation.

I equally congratulate the party and People's Power of Guantánamo, and I congratulate the people of Guantánamo. I ask you to excuse me for omitting many other things I could say to you, due to time considerations.

Fifty years of revolutionary struggle

In 1995, I am also going to complete 50 years of having initiated a long and intense political and revolutionary struggle, which among other things, has allowed me the great privilege of being here with you. It is no longer necessary to make the long speeches of the early years of the revolution.

There is only one thing which I wish to add. The revolution will never renounce its principles. It will never renounce the conquests which it brought to our people, it will never renounce its ideals and objectives, and it will never be forced to its knees before the United States. Our sovereignty will not be surrendered, nor is it negotiable!

The right to construct the social, economic and political regime chosen by our people will not be deposed in the face of anything or anyone! The revolution cannot be destroyed from within or from without.

If we have to fight for a hundred years more, we will fight! Those of us who have had the privilege of experiencing liberty, dignity and justice will never resign ourselves to living without them.

Socialism or death!

Patria o muerte! [Homeland or death!]

Venceremos! [We will win!]

---

[15] José Maceo, younger brother of General Antonio Maceo, was a revolutionary leader in the Ten Years' War (1868–78).

500,000 *Cubans on the streets*

Speech of August 5, 1995

President Fidel Castro spoke at the end of a demonstration in which more than 500,000 people marched along Havana's waterfront, the Malecón, in pouring rain in defense of the revolution on August 5, 1995. At the front of the crowd were the 1,300 youth delegates of the "Cuba Vive" International Youth Festival, a six-day conference organized by the Union of Young Communists of Cuba, the Federation of University Students, the Federation of High School Students and the José Martí Organization of Pioneers.

Fidel commemorates the anniversary of the counterrevolutionary disturbances of August 1994 that led to the "rafters' crisis" and acknowledges the solidarity of the Cuban people in overcoming them and the many other challenges that have confronted Cuba since the revolution. He recognizes the Cuban youth for organizing the massive rally and looks forward to the next world youth festival.

I'm going to begin now, without waiting for you to stir me, so I'll take just a few minutes, and hope that you excuse me. Dear friends from different countries who have visited us in a noble gesture of encouragement; dear compatriots:

You can't hear, right? Well, what can one do? We can't do anything about it. I have a little experience with how events are in places like this. There are still people a kilometer and a half away on this side, and in front they are almost a kilometer away. The site is not ideal for a rally. The crowd is really extraordinary, and I understand it's not easy to communicate with everyone like this, nor was it planned this way. Something else was expected.

That's why I said I came to reflect briefly, because this rally is itself a real miracle! A miracle! Well, believers will say it came from heaven. Those with a different philosophy will say it's a miracle of patriotism and revolutionary spirit of the people. We respect absolutely, as a sacred principle, all beliefs. But it really seemed impossible that this event would occur today, and I say to you that in many years of revolution I have never seen such an uncertain situation regarding a march and rally.

I had planned to join in about 1.7 kilometers from here, at Maceo Park, a place that is symbolic of the events of a year ago. I was thinking of joining there, but on the way I saw such a downpour — not a cloudburst, but a storm — such a deluge that I really didn't think it was possible to maintain and organize such a march. I said to myself, what will the compañeros do? And I said, well, they'll march for sure. I was certain of that. At four o'clock sharp, those who are there will surely set out.

I saw the streets of the Plaza municipality, where the march began, turned into rivers, such a downpour that you couldn't see anything; and I said, well, if 10 people turn out it's already a victory. By my calculation, without exaggerating and, actually, coming up short — Vicky[1] will say no, there are more — at least half a million people have arrived in this march, in these physically unimaginable conditions.

I would have been here among the 10. Of course, I can't even claim credit for having gotten my quota of water, because when I arrived at Maceo Park the rain had let up. But there were people who had been there for a while standing in line, helping to organize, and they were wet, some shivering with cold, because they really got soaked. And it wasn't one downpour, but two intense, very intense, ones! So then, I didn't get my quota of water. What merit can I claim today in this march? None!

What I have had is the privilege of enjoying an occurrence of this nature, which makes us feel really proud of our people; proud of the revolution and its results in the consciousness of the men and

---

[1] Victoria Velázquez is first secretary of the Young Communist Union of Cuba (UJC). She is the first woman to head the UJC.

women of this country; proud of our youth, for being capable of organizing such brilliant events. There are many things; really, I have many reasons for feeling satisfied.

Anniversary of counterrevolutionary disturbances

Vicky was saying, among other things, that we were here today because I had been here last August 5. I came then because I had to come. It was my most elementary duty to be with the people at a moment in which the enemy had worked overtime to create a disturbance. A disturbance! It can't be said it was even an attempt at rebellion; they were simply disturbances. Those disturbances were created around groups that mobilized to hijack boats to travel to the United States, where they were received like heroes.

But they were really carrying out destabilizing activities. By that time one could hardly go to Regla,[2] because someone would pull out a knife, a pistol. They would hijack the Regla boat, or a little, medium-sized or even big boat. They would steal anything, because the bigger the scandal, the better the propaganda against Cuba. And over there [in the United States], they would get extraordinary receptions; they got privileges no citizen in the world gets. All this was with the goal of destabilization, in the midst of a difficult economic situation, in the midst of great sacrifices on the part of our population. And it was those groups that began to create disturbances.

However, following our philosophy that, here, the people are revolutionary and are with the revolution and will be, under any circumstances, we were not going to allow ourselves to be provoked. What is it that the external enemy and their internal allies wanted, even though they were a small minority? They wanted to provoke a bloody confrontation, and they wanted us to use weapons. And we have weapons, weapons for millions of people who are defending the revolution. But we have our weapons to fight external enemies.

Unless they were to land here, unless they were to use arms inside the country against revolutionaries, we have no reason to use weapons, having the people and the masses to maintain the stability of the revolution.

---

[2] Regla is a district in the city of Havana, directly east of Havana Bay. It was from this area that people set out in rafts and other craft for the U.S. during the August 1994 disturbances.

That was my role: to help prevent anyone from being provoked, and we preferred they shoot at us rather than us firing the first shot. And something occurred that had no precedent. In a matter of minutes, the entire people took to the streets and established order. Their massive presence and spirit established order without any use of weapons. Where else in the world does this happen?

Whoever watches television — and everyone does — sees what happens around the world. In civilized, developed Europe; in the United States; in the richest countries, you constantly see crowds of police firing shots and tear gas, beating and kicking people on the ground. This appears every day on television in many countries; and the dead, so many dead, so many injured, so many arrested. It's habitual; it's our daily bread.

That does not happen in Cuba. Oh, but if in Cuba there is the slightest attempt at a disturbance, there is so much propaganda, so much talk everywhere, you would think the revolution was about to collapse.

Some years ago we said this revolution would not fall. Some years back we used an image, that this revolution couldn't be whipped because it was made of steel and wasn't beaten with egg whites — that is to say, it wasn't a meringue. And it's maintained by the support of the people, by the consensus of the people, by the consciousness of the people of what this country was and can never return to. This is true even with their criticisms, or that they protest over everything that they have good reason to protest, or even some who complain due to not having all the information and because we are a people with a rebellious nature.

Nobility of the Cuban people

This is the most noble, sacrificing, selfless, courageous people that one could imagine. It is a people who struggled fiercely for their independence until attaining it; who struggled very hard for justice; who fortunately achieved, with the revolution, a level of culture that is higher than the great majority of countries in the world. It has a high level of education and there are fewer illiterates, for example, than there are in the United States, people who are totally illiterate or those they call "functional illiterates."

This country has many qualities. It has learned and it thinks. This country is writing one of the most glorious pages that has ever been written. When the socialist camp collapsed, when the Soviet Union disappeared, many people in the world believed Cuba would last only days, or at most, weeks. Five years have passed and here it is — and look with what strength!

August 5, 1995, will be remembered too, because this rally has been organized under unimaginable conditions. It hurt me to think of the effort the youth had made to organize this rally during all these days. And at the precise moment when it had begun, these acts of nature happened. I believe anywhere else such a crowd would have broken up, and that didn't happen.

That's why I say that this day, August 5, 1995, will also be historic, and every year it will be our duty to remember the great victory of August 5, 1994, when the people smashed the counterrevolution without firing a shot. This date says a lot, it teaches and inspires a lot, especially because the people are not in the same conditions as 10 years ago, when there was an abundance of many things, so many that we even wasted them — fuel, resources, everything. That is one of the disadvantages of abundance.

Now we have less than half of what we had. Now we find ourselves forced to endure tougher tests, more complex ones. But out of this test, without doubt, we will emerge stronger. Those are the advantages of difficulties.

I am convinced, standing here before this event, that none of us will ever forget what we are seeing here today. I have had the privilege of seeing many gatherings, tests of all kinds in war and peace, the heroism of war and the heroism of peace. But I say this, without reservation, in spite of knowing the problems we have, in spite of knowing there always are those who lack the spirit that is necessary in conditions like these, I believe the people today have more worth, more consciousness and more heroism than ever.

Perhaps some thought they were going to take photos of a line of citizens marching along the Malecón and that 100 drenched people would gather here, dripping wet, and they could say, look how the Cuban revolution is doing! They were not going to talk of the rainstorm, the tempest, the deluge. They were going to say that no one wanted to come to the August 5 rally and that only 100 people came.

What an extraordinary response! We feel the duty, really, to thank our people and the people of our capital. It is precisely in the capital where we have the most problems with housing, water, transportation, electricity and many other things. And see how the people of the capital act!

You who are there below, visitors from 65 countries [at the "Cuba Vive" Festival], you cannot be up here to see what we are seeing. We're happy that you have been able to accompany us on this glorious day.

Truly, I have no words to express our gratitude for the support you have offered us, for this beautiful "Cuba Vive" Youth Festival. I have no words to show our appreciation for the fact that you have accompanied us in such difficult times. And it is appropriate to emphasize that among you are 262 representatives of the people of the United States, because this also tells us about the qualities and virtues of the people of the United States, who are opposed to the unjust and criminal blockade being imposed against Cuba, the likes of which has never been used against any other country, with such rigor and for more than 35 years.

They didn't do this against apartheid, nor against governments in Latin America that disappeared 2,000 or 10,000 or even 30,000 citizens, the location of whose remains is unknown. This was not done against governments that disappeared more than 100,000 citizens in a small country like Guatemala. They do it against Cuba, where there is not one death squad, not one disappearance, not one political assassination in the streets. A country — I say it with all the energy that the truth gives us — where no citizen has ever been tortured. I wonder in which other country the same can be said.

Every day, children are killed; adolescents and children are prostituted in many countries in the region. It is a reality. Every day people take justice into their own hands; every day there are violence, drugs and problems that don't exist in Cuba. Yet we are the only country that is blockaded in the world.

It's for this reason that we must react with great honor and dignity, with a great feeling of patriotism, with all the patience that is necessary, and to wait as long as necessary. We can't have any illusions when extremist elements are dictating policy today in the

United States, wanting to wipe out all social benefits for the people of the United States.

"We can never abandon the struggle"

We can't leave out the possibility that in the future these extremist elements, with the use of all their resources, which are abundant, might gain total power in the United States, could have total reign, for four, eight or 12 more years. If these extremist elements succeed and gain control, not only of the Senate but of the government, it will mean for us new periods of danger, of risk, of blockades, and that's why it's not an exaggeration to say that if we have to fight a hundred more years, we will fight a hundred more years.

Our country has struggled more than a hundred years for its independence — quite a bit more than a hundred years — against attempts to annex us, to swallow us, to devour us. We can never abandon that struggle, and we won't abandon it! Time does not matter. In this we have to have more patience than the Chinese. In this we have to act, one might say, with the wisdom of a thousand-year-old people.

And I am sure that neither this generation nor those that follow — that is, neither the youth of today nor the youth of tomorrow — will renounce that glorious struggle, not only for independence and freedom but for equality and justice. Our people will never renounce those aspirations!

We neither exaggerate nor dramatize when we say we're ready to struggle as long as necessary. Yes, we should do things better and better, and we're obligated to do them better each time, to be more efficient, to be more dedicated to our obligations, to our duty, to our beloved and heroic people, to learn all the lessons from these difficult times.

Vicky was telling me some of our visitors' impressions when you saw, for example, the Computer Center, or the rehabilitation schools, the schools for the disabled, the child-care centers, the family doctors, the hospitals, the efforts this country makes to sustain all this; and how, in spite of having lost 70 percent of our imports, not a single school has been closed, nor a hospital; nor is there a single child without medical care, nor a child without a teacher.

What excuse can those who have such great resources — billions and billions — find or use when they haven't been able to solve even one of these problems? Capitalism has been unable to solve even one of these problems.

There are countries that have endless amounts of oil, mineral resources, reserves in the banks, and they cannot show any of the things that our people, in a special period and under a blockade, can show.

Just think of what we could do, the day the blockade ends, the day they leave us in peace? We will struggle for that day and wait for that day, and your confidence will not be betrayed. Your love and encouragement will not be in vain; the seed you plant in our hearts will never be lost.

We will continue to count on you and on the millions and millions of people like you who, fortunately, exist around the world. We will continue to count on that support from all parts.

The youth will meet again

The youth of the world will return one day to meet again, and if they don't meet somewhere else, or if no country makes itself available for a festival organized like this one, then a world festival can be organized. What's lacking is not money. What is needed is modesty, generosity, goodwill, like that of those families who hosted you, like that of the neighborhoods that welcomed you and greeted you everywhere. Millions are not needed, and it can be organized like this festival, in which each person did their part and paid for their own trip.

After this experience, if the world festivals don't continue, then here in Cuba, under a special period and a blockade, we have enough generosity, common sense and organizational capacity to hold an event of this kind.

It's not that we're proposing it here. They told me it was going to be in South Africa, but that it wasn't possible. Reactionaries don't like such festivals. Right-wing extremists and hegemonists don't like them, and for that reason not many people are concerned whether there are youth festivals.

But what a beautiful event this is, what experiences it leaves us — the method, the style, the meetings in the provinces. Cuba is bigger yet, and a festival can reach Baracoa, Santiago de Cuba, Holguín, in all parts, with or without a hurricane, because a storm went around the Youth Festival, but it behaved well, it headed north. It's not that we wanted it to pass by Florida. It would have been better if it had turned back earlier and gone toward the Atlantic. But, well, it left us with the water, and you, too; because I believe you were greeted with water, and today you got wet. So you probably are returning to your countries a little bigger, having grown like our sugarcane, which is growing now with the water and the heat.

Many thanks. Thank you very much, dear guests. Cuba lives and will live as long as there are men and women like you in the world, as long as there is a people as heroic as ours, capable of defending that right to life!

How much I liked, once again, that slogan Vicky proclaimed here so beautifully:

Socialism or death!

Patria o muerte! [Homeland or death!]

Venceremos! [We shall win!]

Now we give the stage over to the musicians, whom we almost forgot, so that the whole country can enjoy their magnificent art, those who are here and those at home. A speech can't be listened to for more than half an hour, but good music, good art can be enjoyed all afternoon and all night.

Thank you.

"Cuba Vive"
International Youth Festival

Speech of August 6, 1995

President Fidel Castro spoke at the closing ceremony of the "Cuba Vive" International Youth Festival, held at the Karl Marx Theater in Havana on August 6, 1995.

It seems to me, in all honesty, that there is nothing left to say here. Everything has already been said, and expressed much better than I could have expressed it. But I was put under great pressure by the organizers, and Vicky [UJC leader Victoria Velázquez] in particular, to come here and say a few words and, as a further inconvenience, with a voice that has practically gone on strike. What shall we do? We can't start throwing tear gas bombs at it or try to put it down with pumpers and all those devices we see used every day in other parts of the world. So I will have to carry on regardless, and try to accomplish the task as well as possible.

There are two groups here today: one that has been here all day and is familiar with the issues covered, what has been said, that is, the arguments, the ideas put forward; and another which wasn't here during the day.

We are also honored with the presence of the diplomatic corps. What a headache it must be to be a member of the diplomatic corps at an event like this! I know from experience because if they applaud, it is reported that they applauded. If they don't applaud, it is reported that they didn't applaud. If people get to their feet and they remain seated, it's reported: The diplomatic corps remained seated. That is precisely what happened when you started to shout "Cuba Lives!" and, of course, out of discipline, the diplomats remained in their seats, though I am sure that none of them would want Cuba not to live.

In his speech this afternoon, Robertico [Robaina] really gave a brilliant explanation of the fundamental ideas and concepts related to our revolution in the present context. I think Vicky's speech was magnificent as well, and very few chinks are left to fill in this evening.

Global challenges confront the youth

I would rather reflect on the world that is yours to live in, the young people represented here and to whom my words are principally addressed. In our view — that is to say, in the view of revolutionaries and people who are not pessimistic, we can't afford to be — it is a very difficult world.

The approach of the year 2000 and another century is spoken of joyfully. That is only natural; the last thing human beings lose is hope. But as we see things, it seems that the new generations that you represent, in Cuba and the whole world, will have to tackle very serious problems on all fronts. I am not just talking here about environmental issues. Really, for the first time, the possibility of the world surviving the destruction that is taking place in the natural environment and to humanity's ways of living has been questioned, an issue that has been much talked about. However, the effects are becoming increasingly obvious, visible and worrying.

For example, for a few years now there has been talk about the famous greenhouse effect, the ozone layer and other such problems. However, we are already experiencing the greenhouse effect. Cuba is experiencing it, we are aware of it, the world is witness to what is happening. Terrible heat waves all over the place; nearly 1,000 people died from heat exposure in the United States, as they have in England, in almost all parts of Europe, everywhere.

According to records, the last few years have been the hottest for a hundred years. We are already seeing the consequences of these effects, but they are by no means the worst we are going to see.

There are strange atmospheric phenomena of all kinds. We have just had the case of a cyclone or hurricane which, while passing through Florida, caused some extremely heavy rainfall in our country, from hundreds of kilometers away.

We have had recent proof of man's destruction and overexploitation of natural resources in the conflict which arose between Canada and the European Union over the Atlantic halibut species. We know of it since we have heard a lot about this virtual fishing war during the last few months.

The number of fishing zones, not only there but also in the South Atlantic, are fast being exhausted; and yet the world population is already approaching six billion inhabitants. By the famous year 2000 the world population will already have reached the six billion mark, if I am not mistaken, because I have three of those devices, given to me as presents, which you can sit in front of and see how the population is growing per second and per minute.

The phenomenon of drought is being experienced all over the world; either severe drought or excessive rainfall — tremendous floods in China — that causes so much damage, that kills thousands of people in other parts of the world, or long months without rainfall. It has been confirmed that sea levels are rising every year.

What I want to say is that humanity is clearly starting to experience the effects of the destruction of the environment. It is horrifying to hear of the number of species being destroyed, from both the plant and animal worlds, every day throughout the world; and it's perceptible, the phenomenon is visible. There is no doubt that this growing population will have to confront massive ecological problems, and you will be witnesses to that.

But I would like to refer fundamentally to another aspect of the issue, the political aspect, the social aspect. Will the coming century, so much talked about, be the century of unipolar hegemony, the domination of world politics by one single country or group of countries? Will it be the century of economic globalization, of the outright triumph of the transnationals and the imposition of a new world order far worse than the one we have today?

What will be left in this world for the countries that constitute the overwhelming majority of humanity? What guarantees do they have, what security? Will they by any chance be able to compete with the latest and most developed technology? Where will their markets be? What will be the prices of their products? What place will they have in the world? And this issue is not only about the countries formerly referred to as the Third World. It is also about countries which were not viewed as being part of the Third World — the Soviet Union and ex-socialist bloc countries — which have, in effect, now become part of the Third World in terms of their economic indices, gross domestic product, their competitiveness, their ability to find markets; and as such, have increased the number, we could say, of the world's poor.

Agreement has just been reached on the norms that should regulate international trade as laid down in the Uruguay Round, the GATT — currently the WTO[1] — and already, in practice, big powers are beginning to ignore these norms. We have seen the methods used by the United States to resolve its differences with Europe and Japan, threats of trade wars, extremely high tariff barriers, through which it is imposing its conditions on the rest of the world, including the developed world.

Neoliberalism: dangers and consequences

New theories have arisen. The order of the day is no longer imperialism, which is almost as old as Methuselah, we could say, in its modern form; although the world has already known an empire in the past which lasted for many years, the Roman Empire whose Capitol, I believe, served as a model for the Capitol of the present-day empire which is the United States.

During the Cuban revolutionary process which began in 1959, people spoke of imperialism, colonialism and neocolonialism. On the international scene there was much talk about these ideas, these concepts; they were studied, analyzed. Now the reference is neo-

---

[1] The World Trade Organization (WTO) was created in the Uruguay Round of the General Agreement on Tariffs and Trade (GATT). GATT was formed in 1947 by the industrialized countries to regulate and control international trade. The Uruguay Round (1986–92) vastly increased GATT's scope and established WTO to oversee its global dominance over resources and the flow of investments, and maintain monopoly control of technology. WTO's officials are unelected and their decision-making will take place in secret, with neither public participation nor review. Their decisions will be binding on governments, without respect for their sovereignty or public policy.

liberalism, and some claim that the coming century will be the century of neoliberalism.

In fact, when the socialist camp and the Soviet Union collapsed, all these imperialist theories made great advances. In reality, the time had come to settle accounts, to take control of the world economy, and all the international credit institutions and the developed world imposed neoliberal policies. We are already beginning to see the consequences.

I do not find it very pleasant to mention countries by name, nor do I want to offend anyone of those present here, or the representatives of certain countries. You referred to them this morning. The monstrous consequences of neoliberalism are already appearing in many parts of the world.

Barely two years ago other problems were being discussed: the social problems resulting from neoliberalism. The universal complaint of teachers, doctors and professionals who attended congresses here in Cuba was the suppression of credits and the budgets allocated to education, health care, social security, social development, for all those activities. But the economic crisis of neoliberalism could still not be seen clearly, that crisis which is now being manifested in the form of high unemployment figures, which in some regions have tripled in scarcely two years, or serious financial problems which could ruin any country overnight. There are also countries with vast natural resources and huge incomes, which are on the verge of a social explosion resulting from daily battles between workers, the police and other repressive forces, in Central America, in South America and in other places. We are already seeing the consequences, and there are countries which have clearly stated that they are not going toward neoliberalism, that they are going to avoid it at all cost.

Friends of ours, important figures, have sent messages to us saying: "We do not know where you are headed" — good question, and linked to some of the concerns raised here — "but we advise you not to go where we are going." These are the words of friends who are caught up in this war of neoliberalism, and are now committed to that policy.

The effects are already such that even international organizations such as the IMF and the World Bank are talking of social development and of giving credits for social development. They are beginning to take serious note of the time bomb that is ticking away everywhere, and in Latin America in particular. In spite of all this talk of macroeconomic indices, everyday reality is confronting them; it is a terrible and desperate situation.

Everything has to be privatized! Well, they have already privatized almost everything. They solved budget deficits with the revenue from privatizations, but the state's private properties are now gone; properties built up over decades are fast disappearing in the name of that practice and that philosophy. Soon there will be nothing left to privatize.

One of the results of such privatizations — I was reading about it in a recent wire dispatch — in a South American country where an aircraft factory was privatized, was that a transnational came along and its first move was to reduce the number of workers in that industry from 1,200 to 400. It can't be said that they are going to solve the problem of unemployment in this way.

Now neoliberal theoreticians are trying to work out how to combat unemployment, in the same way that the large banking institutions are discussing what to do in terms of social development. But the fundamental problem is this: capitalism and social development always have been, always are, and always will be irreconcilable. Capitalism and plunder, plunder within and outside the country, are inseparable. Capitalism and unemployment are inseparable; try to tell Europe it's any different.

There are countries in Europe with more than 20 percent unemployment, and the famous industrial restructuring as a means of increasing competitiveness has brought further unemployment. Certain countries in Europe have been forced to uproot thousands of olive trees, producing an excellent cholesterol-free oil, something the rich are very concerned about these days; the poor virtually lack those cholesterol problems.

Millions of grapevines, millions of hectares of land left uncultivated; subsidies given to campesinos so that they do not produce food; millions of head of cattle sacrificed to increase the milk prices; FAO[2] statements on the fall in cereal production, implying an increase in the prices of all the cereals bought by Third World coun-

---

[2] FAO is the Food and Agriculture Organization of the United Nations, based in Rome.

tries, because as is well known, wheat is not grown in tropical countries. Corn is also produced under very different conditions. That is nothing new for Cubans; we have to cope with cyclones, droughts, plagues, etc. Cereals are mainly produced in temperate climates. Only rice, which is low in protein, grows easily in the tropics.

Slaughtering animals means starving people to death, destroying plantations, limiting and subsidizing the nonproduction of grains. Where is the logic behind all this in a growing world which is enduring increasingly greater food problems? This is not good news for the poor countries of the world.

What would happen if NAFTA covered all the Latin American countries, if they were yoked to the economy of the United States? No one knows the consequences that could have! But there are countries that historically have cultivated corn that will no longer be producing it, because now the crop is produced more cheaply in the United States, and they can't compete with U.S. corn. In this way, a whole series of mechanisms and plans are being interlinked, designed to serve the interests of the world's most developed nation, which already has a hundred times greater development than the other countries of the world; opportunities to compete, the experience to compete, ultra-modern technology, financial resources to offer credits, which all the other countries lack. This is a problem which they will have to confront in the near future; they are already facing it.

In the information field, as you mentioned in one of the commissions, the production of audiovisual material for the entertainment industry is currently monopolized almost exclusively by the United States, which has practically taken over the European market and that of the rest of the world. Some of their productions, as we know, are good, but there is a huge volume of poison in every shape and form.

Many U.S. citizens are becoming alarmed at the quantity of violence being generated, inspired by those television programs containing violence and sexual abuse, as has already been said. Legislation is being discussed and technical mechanisms are even being invented to oversee the selection of films, and how to create a system in every household so that certain movies can't be viewed — it must be very complicated. I believe the television networks can do this with the sole aid of electronics and computers; they have an extraordinary technical advantage at their disposal. They are worried, but who's worried about us, what they transmit to us, what they sell us?

Now there's talk of information highways, new aspects that, through their propaganda and influences on the human mentality, will serve to prop up the economic order they want to impose on the world. These are important changes that have taken place which we have had the privilege of observing during these 36 years of revolution.

The world being designed has no future

But it is a real fact that solid foundations do exist to support the conviction that the world that is being designed for us in the next century has no future whatsoever. It will enter into crisis, it will have to enter into crisis, and it will be in that world where you will have to try to take forward the ideas contained in the commission reports on education, health, the environment, women, children, culture, employment, democracy and participation. And I'm not telling you these things to discourage you, far from it, but to give you full credit for the questions you have raised here; because it can safely be said that in this International Youth Festival you have drawn up a program of work and struggle, and an inventory of the problems in the world today.

Added to this, there are clear indications in certain important countries of a political shift to the right, a turning toward reactionary positions, not everywhere, but in a few very important countries, among them the United States, which plays a decisive role in the world of today and will inevitably play it in the world of tomorrow. There is a tremendous shift which has shocked those who at some time or other received news and information on the big crisis of the 1930s, Roosevelt's efforts of the time to save capitalism, the socially oriented measures to reduce unemployment, to improve people's living conditions, their education and health care.

It must be said, there have been struggles within the United States itself, over several years, which led to a series of social conquests: the black population's battle for their rights, a historic battle; the national minorities' struggles; and the struggles of the unemployed, of the poor and of women to win a series of advances. Today, all this is clearly in danger as a consequence of the shift to the right in U.S. politics, to the extent of reaching really extreme right-wing positions.

Every day wire dispatches report on an agreement in the U.S. Congress to overturn some measure, some act, some budget, or resources across the board. Nobody knows how long the U.S. population will stand for this, but a war is being waged against social gains. Even the affirmative action programs, measures adopted to protect the weakest and most vulnerable sectors in society, so that they could obtain jobs and certain benefits, they also want to do away with those affirmative action programs.

This would need a lengthy explanation, but super-reactionary forces, spawned throughout the Cold War period, have emerged, with a very reactionary political thinking which has tremendous force and tremendous resources, and this explains those phenomena taking place in the United States, which today is not a model to follow, far be it, but which could be far worse than it is. This is the country that has blockaded us over all these years.

The extreme right could come to have almost total control of power in the United States. This is a factor which is very important to keep in mind, because the world situation could worsen and U.S. imperialism could become more aggressive and much more dangerous for the world.

Suffice it to say that, in relation to the United Nations, there are currently two theories: one held by those who want to use the United Nations as an instrument to "sanctify" their interventions in any part of the globe and their foreign policy, but hiding behind a fig leaf, which is the United Nations — it's now called the United Nations but it wasn't always like this — and those who want to make it disappear so as to exercise direct power in the world, those who want to get rid of the stumbling block of the United Nations. These are two schools, I repeat: one, those who want to use it as an instrument; the other, those who want to make it disappear because they see it as a stumbling block. These are the theories that are being discussed.

Attacks on Cuba from without and within

In relation to Cuba, two political theories are also under discussion: the one of those people who wish to destroy us from outside — that is to say, with more hostility, with more threats of aggression — and that of the "noble and generous gentlemen" who want to destroy us from within, but both of them using the blockade; both theories are supported by the blockade.

However, some people think this blockade is enough, but we have to add this and that to destabilize and destroy the revolution; as if we were fools or sucked our thumbs, because the famous Torricelli Act's "track two" could have some potentiality and some effect on stupid people. You don't even have to be a genius to know that we can't be caught by that policy, and in the same way we have to have sufficient serenity to resist the other variant.

If we found out tomorrow that the extreme right had conquered not only the U.S. Congress, but also the U.S. government, this wouldn't scare us. We have already been through similar periods, although it could be worse in terms of hostility and threats from abroad. And, as Vicky said, none of those factors dishearten us. But they remain theories; there are theories for the world and theories for Cuba.

It seems Cuba has become important, given that we are the only country to be blockaded by the United States. In relation to our country the harshest restrictions are being maintained. They can have completely different ideas on any other country, but as far as Cuba is concerned they are not giving in yet. Because of this we have been resisting for 35 years, and I also said that we have to be prepared to resist for another 35 years or longer. Really, our country has fought for almost 130 years in defense of its independence, and I believe that the values handed down to us by our forebears are very present in our people.

It is appropriate for our friends throughout the world to know that, and also that our people know it, and our people do know it. And since we are optimists, I am certain that there are reserves within the people, reserves within the country. It is possible for our country to resist, and even to continue to move forward.

Lessons from Guatemala

When I say we have to resist, examples of what has happened in some other countries always come to mind, and I am going to recall one, making an exception: what happened in Guatemala in 1954, already 41 years ago.

Guatemala had a revolutionary political movement, which represented a hope for Latin America and Central America. The Guatemalan people had hope through an agrarian reform law and certain social measures, and a mercenary expedition like that of the Bay of Pigs was immediately organized in the United States.

The country was invaded. The Guatemalan revolutionaries had no chance to defend themselves and to crush that invasion. A representative government was established, organized and created by the CIA and the U.S. government. During these 41 years, in that country of less than 10 million inhabitants — there may be that number now, the population must have doubled in 41 years — an incredible total of over 100,000 persons have disappeared. That was the result of the mercenary victory.

What would have happened to Cuba if the Bay of Pigs invasion had been successful in 1961? What would have become of this country if we'd had to endure a victorious counterrevolution? The history of the Paris Commune would be tame in comparison.[3] All Cubans know what ceasing to fight, ceasing to resist, would signify, and we know perfectly well what it would mean. I think that yesterday was an objective proof of that, the spirit shown yesterday by our people here in the capital, where we have greater difficulties.

Now think about it. And this is no secret, because the famous Helms-Burton bill, yet another on the list, aggressive, repugnant, is so brutal that it virtually threatens our country — as [Ricardo] Alarcón has explained on various occasions — with depriving the people of everything they have. They will be left with virtually no schools, no day-care centers, no special education centers, no hospitals and no family doctors. When they come to apply the measure they have demanded of other countries, it is possible that 100 percent of family doctors will be jobless, because how and for what will they be paid?

---

[3] The Paris Commune was an insurrection of radical Parisians against the pro-royalist National Assembly in March–May 1871. While the Commune was not a socialist revolution, it was unique in that it granted unprecedented control of all institutions to the workers. In the May counterrevolution, the Commune was brutally crushed by 130,000 troops sent in by the Assembly in a week of bloody street fighting. More than 17,000 people were executed in subsequent reprisals.

Practically all the agricultural workers of this country would lose their lands, except some who already owned land, since the overwhelming majority own land because the revolution gave it to them. All the UBPCs,[4] all the cooperative workers would lose everything they have.

In a country such as Cuba, where 85 percent of families own their homes, by virtue of the revolution's laws and work, all those families would lose their ownership. The whole thing is so ludicrous that we were almost at the point of sending a telegram of thanks to Helms and Burton, saying, "Oh, by the way, thanks very much; just look how you are helping us."

· According to the Helms-Burton bill, as Clinton himself has said, compensation payable by Cuba on former U.S. properties would amount to more than $5 or $6 billion. It would have to be argued, moreover, as this is not our figure. And even if we were to accept it, it does not take into account the tens of billions of dollars they owe us in compensation due to the blockade. If we received compensation, we would even be prepared to pay out on U.S. properties. I was going to tell you that, according to Clinton's calculations, this bill demands payments of $100 billion, taking into account properties belonging to Cubans who subsequently became U.S. citizens, and according to the bill, the blockade will continue until the $100 billion are paid. It seems that they are realizing this and some people are beginning to talk of a few modifications being made to its monstrous contents. But for us the result is exactly the same. We are fully aware of what it would signify if this country were to fall once again into the hands of the United States, with or without the Helms-Burton bill. Reports of what happened in Indonesia would pale into insignificance, and in Guatemala, not worth thinking about.

---

[4] UBPCs, translated, means Basic Units of Cooperative Production. Created in 1993, UBPCs represent a new agricultural form created to increase food production through incentives to cooperatives. Land is owned by the state, and farm implements and equipment can be purchased by the collective. After the agreed-upon production quota, set to meet the population's needs, is met by the UBPC, the cooperative's members can sell the surplus produce. Much of state farmland has been converted to UBPCs.

Cubans will not be slaves

However, the ultimate, the inconceivable, is to believe that Cubans would act like the slaves who were taken to the Roman circus and who shouted: "Long live Caesar! We who are going to die salute you!" As if one Cuban here would be prepared to say: "Long live the emperor!" or "Long live the empire! We who are going to die are going to bow down our heads so that you can wipe us out!"

They have to know that everyone here would take up arms and fight until the death, until a truly glorious death. What is ignominious is for someone to place their head on the chopping block for the United States to cut it off. They realize that this cannot and will never happen, despite the idiotic things they say — so contemptuous! They should have learned something from all the years of Cuban resistance and struggle, because we will never accept that fate.

You, our friends, can understand that we have solid and profound reasons for thinking as we do. But if it wasn't a question of defending the lives of the citizens of this country, if it was only about defending the ideas that the revolution defends, it would be worthwhile to fight once and a thousand times to the death.

At a certain point in history the Christians were the first communists — because, as the Bible tells us, the early Christians, as we have read and were told so many times, were sent to the circus, to be devoured by the lions. They allowed themselves to be devoured without renouncing their Christian faith. We will not be lesser than they, because we believe that the values signified by the ideas that we are defending are comparable to the best ideas for which people have been prepared to die, and we will always prefer to die rather than to renounce our revolutionary faith.

The revolution is our religion, which does not exclude anyone, including revolutionaries, from holding another. We are not expecting any reward, because I believe that being a revolutionary — as Che said — is the highest level humanity can attain.

Revolutionaries do not expect anything in return, which means that revolutionaries have to dedicate themselves totally to a cause, to their ideas, to their noble objectives, without expecting anything in return. I would say, without in any way diminishing any other conviction, that this is really what makes a genuine revolutionary conviction, the noblest and deepest conviction which has ever existed.

I'm referring to the revolutionary and communist conviction; I'm not talking about other convictions. I am genuinely talking to you from the heart.

The necessity of market economic reforms

This leads on to some of the issues which have been mentioned here and which have worried you, which I partly covered on July 26, concerning what we are doing and how we are doing it.

Comrade José Luis[5] had the disagreeable and difficult role of explaining what we are doing and how we are going about it, in the economic terrain, in order to move forward.

Vicky told me that many of our visitors were anxious about the risks inherent in the measures that we are taking. This concern is expressed clearly in a paragraph in one of the resolutions.

I believe that those who are worried have reason to be, in the first place because it is a worrying issue. What effect will these market openings, these measures we are taking, have on the future of the revolution? As a consequence of all this, are we going to be different in the future, are these measures going to corrupt us?

I have said that we are introducing elements of capitalism into our system, into our economy. This is a fact. We have also discussed the consequences we have observed from the employment of those mechanisms. Yes, we are doing this.

I have already spoken to you about the world we are living in. Don't forget that we are an island surrounded on all sides, even from above, by capitalism; let's say from outer space, which is full of satellites and goodness knows what else, over which we have absolutely no control. You can be sure that if a dog goes to the park to do its business, the U.S. satellites will be aware of the fact, will observe it and take photos of it.

They have the world surrounded by satellites spying on everything. Of course, this makes them the masters of the communication systems. If we talked over the telephone with some country and said things that shouldn't be said over the phone, we would be big fools. There is no official telephone call from this country that is not picked up by them. The same applies to conversations with political

---

[5] José Luis Rodríguez is Minister of Finance and Prices.

leaders or with important companies. They monitor everything, because the blockade is much more than a prohibition on buying and selling. You can't possibly imagine the extent of it. The blockade is a neverending persecution levied against any commercial activity the country attempts to engage in.

With the capitalists who visit us here — as I recently said, some come with their corrupting habits, but many are serious capitalists. I mean that they don't try to bribe or cheat people. They argue; you have to argue a lot with them, because, logically, it is the law of capitalism. Every business deal is tightly argued — you have to speak softly and whisper in their ears and say: "Listen, don't talk on the telephone to another country about this."

I don't know to how many people we've given this advice and they don't take any notice. They make a phone call, send a fax, etc., and a few days later the U.S. ambassador, or the consul or an official is paying them a visit — usually it's the ambassador.

When they are aware of any negotiations we're having, don't think for one moment that it's easy. Pay no heed. It wouldn't be so easy for us to take the capitalist road because the Yankees would take it upon themselves to prevent us; they don't want that. When I say Yankee I am using the word in a pejorative sense, referring to those who wish us harm, never as a means of describing the U.S. people.

They do not want us to do any business, nor invest in anything, nor have access to credits, nor to privatize anything. They don't want any of that — we are perfectly aware that all they want is our head and they have not even bothered to discuss the price. But the blockade is very serious. It is an unending persecution which makes everything more expensive. We have to look for merchandise thousands of miles away. The ships cannot make stopovers in any U.S. port, so transportation is more expensive. Short-term commercial credits are extremely expensive, everything difficult for Cuba. This is what the blockade means; really it is much more than it seems. And, of course, it is putting obstacles in the way of these measures which we are taking and which we have to take.

Actually, if we were one of those countries with abundant natural resources, and they do exist, and which have millions or billions of dollars in the banks of the developed countries, because they have easy access to capital. . . .

For example, we know what it is to produce one ton of sugar, when you have to sweat to do it. Of course, when the revolution triumphed, one ton of sugar bought — I don't want to get this wrong — about seven or eight tons of oil at least. So that means that, at the price sugar had at the triumph of the revolution, we could satisfy the country's entire oil requirements from the sale of one million tons.

Now, during these years of the special period, sometimes we have only been able to buy 1.4 tons of oil for one ton of sugar. That's almost putting sugar and oil on a par, and look at the hard labor that goes into producing one ton of sugar! In many places, including at sea, the transnationals arrive and succeed in setting up oil production at really low costs in areas of high yields.

The oil crisis has affected very few countries in the world to the extent that it has affected Cuba, and today the bulk of the country's exports are devoted to buying oil. That's to say, circumstances are not easy for us; we are putting a lot of effort into exploring for oil; we are looking for national sources.

The special period came about as part of the country's defense plans for war situations: what to do if there was a total blockade imposed on Cuba by the United States and nothing could enter; how we could survive under those conditions. It is called "special period" in wartime; but the collapse of the socialist camp and the Soviet Union obliged us to experience the special period during peacetime, because, abruptly, almost overnight, all trade with the socialist bloc and with the Soviet Union disappeared.

Prior to this, they were paying us reasonable prices for our sugar and they were not the only ones. Even the Lomé Convention does not pay for sugar at the world market rate; it pays at a much higher rate. We call the world sugar market the sugar waste bin, where all sugar is sold very cheaply. The United States itself previously used to buy Cuban sugar, and then, as a reprisal, they reduced to zero the three million or so annual tons they bought from us. They pay for their sugar quotas at a slightly higher price. We have to sell our sugar at world market prices.

From one day to the next we lost all our oil supplies, all our supplies of raw material, of foodstuffs, of spare parts for our factory machinery which came from the socialist bloc. This has happened to us twice in our history: When the U.S. blockade started nearly all our machinery and motor transport were of U.S. origin, and now the same thing is happening again, because what we have suffered is a double blockade. U.S. pressure on the former socialist countries was such that it has resulted in trade being suspended almost 100 percent. We had to cope with this overnight, by ourselves, without a single cent from any world banking institution such as the Inter-American Bank, the World Bank or the IMF. Absolutely no one! We had to manage with what we had.

As was said a short while ago, we lost 70 percent of the country's imports, and a country that had supplied electricity to over 90 percent of the population was suddenly left with 40 percent of its fuel requirements. I don't know if there is any other country in Latin America or in the world that could have resisted the massive blow that Cuba received, and this with an intensified blockade; because while we had good economic relations with the socialist camp and with the Soviet Union, we were able to defend ourselves much better against the blockade, producing sugar and various other products in a context of increased trade with those countries, which was abruptly lost.

Can you believe that the people of any Latin American country, or anywhere in the world, could have survived such a blow? For how many days, or weeks, if at all? Could a different kind of society be able to do so? This is also related to another question on political themes approached in the commission on democracy and participation. Could Cuba have resisted without its socialist system, without the political and economic system existing in our country when this occurred?

I talked to you before about the economic question, so it's better to continue on this theme. We lost all opportunity for obtaining capital for investments, technology, our markets, we lost all our markets. In fact, what would a genuine revolution have done under those circumstances? What should a Marxist-Leninist revolution have done? We have no fear of pronouncing this word.

What would Marx say?
We could ask ourselves: what would Marx have said? It's almost certain that he would have said: "Listen, don't take it upon yourselves to make a socialist revolution in a Third World country. Wait until

capitalism has been fully developed and then, when the forces of production and all the rest have been developed, the moment will come for making the socialist revolution." This is perhaps what Marx would have said to us. Of course, we would have to see what he would have said if we'd asked him what to do, after we'd already made a socialist revolution here, right on the doorstep of the United States. I believe he would have said: "Fine, I'm happy to have had such outstanding disciples over there in the Caribbean."

You are all aware that the whole question of whether socialism in one country is possible or not has been amply discussed; or if it is possible once the revolution has broken out in the most industrialized countries, in relation to Germany, England or in the European nations. This was discussed over many, many years; but Marxism didn't stop with Marx, and the doctrines of socialism moved on from Marx and Engels. Other great figures came along, great personalities in political and revolutionary thinking. There was Lenin, and it has to be said that Lenin and those who made the October Revolution all believed that the European revolution was a prerequisite for creating socialism. When the European revolution didn't take place, then came the moment when they took the decision that had to be made: "Well, we can't surrender; we have to create socialism in one country."

Of course, talking of one country is relative, given that it was one country of 22 million square kilometers. We are one country of 111,111 square kilometers, according to a geographer, so that the young people will remember Cuba's land surface area in square kilometers — and the construction of socialism was begun, in the midst of a blockade, the enormous historic feat of building socialism in one country. But Lenin was already thinking of the revolution in China, and revolution in the colonized countries. Marxist thought gave him a tremendous impetus and enrichment. And indeed, a force was created which fulfilled an extraordinary role in the world, and served as a balance.

The capitalist world, terrified by socialist ideas, began to be concerned about social problems, about the situation of the workers, etc., concerns that never troubled them before. The services lent to the world by the existence of the socialist camp, and particularly the Soviet Union, are not known.

Recently the end of World War II was commemorated, and in fact, the whole world should remember and did remember that the Soviet Union lost 27 million people in that war. I will go further and say that, without socialism, the Nazi regime would have taken power in the world within a period of time impossible to precisely estimate. This is down to historians to conjecture; but really, it was that socialist country which checked them, which destroyed Hitler's best armored and motorized divisions, and the country that offered resistance — the facts are irrefutable — because when the tanks appeared behind the Soviet lines, the people continued to fight.

In that war which was initiated with new techniques and tactics, resistance collapsed within a matter of weeks. Let's say that the English resisted the bombings, which were very heavy, and entrenched themselves behind the maritime barrier with its powerful squadron. Other countries lacking a natural barrier of this nature and those means of protection were invaded and controlled. Let's mention the noble people of Yugoslavia who also fought so hard against Hitler's divisions, that Yugoslavia which today is destroyed and caught up in an absurd war, incomprehensible, apparently insoluble, victim really of the longing to dissolve everything smelling of socialism.

The Soviet Union resisted, which I believe was a great feat, and we know the story of all the errors and all the barbarities — to put it in strong language — that were perpetrated in that process, ranging from the personality cult to terror, abuses of power and forced collectivization.

Destruction of the Soviet Union

Socialism needed to be perfected, not destroyed. The only countries that stood to gain from the destruction of socialism were the imperialist countries. At first it was a big celebration, but now many Western politicians are afraid because they don't know what's going on over there. It's a Third World country, an exporter of raw materials, with extremely powerful nuclear weapons and with great internal risks, as we have seen very recently. For what? I believe that peace and disarmament had been fought for, and I think that a wiser world would have sought to achieve via negotiations what could have been attained without the dissolution and disintegration of the Soviet Union.

It was said here that this occurred because of errors within the model. It wasn't only that — it can't be described in one word — they allowed themselves to be infiltrated from within. They allowed themselves to be influenced by the propaganda of the consumer society, forgetting that for centuries this was the fruit of colonialism and the plunder of the peoples. They allowed themselves to be blinded by capitalism, and there were many people who believed that any day they would be living like people in Paris, London, all those places; that's the reality. We are now seeing the results. There was ingenuousness, incompetence, a total recipe for the destruction of that which millions of Hitler's soldiers were unable to destroy, to destroy that which cost 27 million lives in the war. The objectives and ideals for which they fought were well worth saving.

I say that peace was conceivable, but of course there was competition between the United States and the Soviet Union in terms of the arms race. And today everyone knows that Reagan's strategy was to ruin the Soviet Union, by imposing on it an arms race which was beyond its economic potential.

It wasn't only the Soviet leaders who were mistaken. World leaders were also at fault, because they were incapable of fighting for a real peace without breaking up entire countries, the consequences of which are still unknown. For the moment, it constitutes tremendous hardships for the world economy, which has to find tens of additional billions every year to try to salvage the situation there, without anyone knowing exactly what is going to happen.

In the former Soviet Union we now have the situation where an economy, which was being formed over more than 70 years, collapsed. Without doubt it will recover one day. The desire to recreate, albeit only a common market, can be seen in many of the countries that formed part of the Soviet Union, not exactly in all of them — very strong nationalist sentiments and hatred have been unleashed in some of the countries.

But the fact is, as I told you, that we have lost a market, we lost our trade, we lost everything, and, in all events, we had to find a solution.

I was speaking of this when I asked how Marx would have responded, and now I'm asking how Lenin would have responded, and I'm sure that Lenin would have said to us: "Do what you're doing, continue doing what you are doing." This is why I said on July 26 that a true Marxist-Leninist will do what we are doing.

They had to do it. They had to move toward a new economic policy, the famous NEP,[6] during one historic period. But there is something more. At certain points Lenin also planted the idea of building capitalism under proletarian leadership. For your peace of mind, of course, I can tell you that we are not thinking of doing anything of the kind. And it's not because we are in disagreement with Lenin, but because circumstances are different, since our process, which was able to rely on assistance from the socialist camp and from the Soviet Union, has made great advances. It has very strong forces and does not have to raise the question in those terms.

I have already said, or tried to tell you before, that if we were a country with significant oil or similar resources, perhaps we wouldn't have gone for large-scale tourism development. From experience, we know all the consequences of large-scale tourism development. However, given the existing conditions in our country, we couldn't do without it, since given those conditions we couldn't do without foreign investment.

Although prior to the collapse of the socialist camp we were considering certain forms of foreign investment for joint enterprises in certain sectors where there was no other solution, we are well aware that over several years we fought against foreign investments, that over several years we felt proud of the fact that the people were the owners of all their resources, of all their industries and all the country's wealth. However, given the existing conditions, we couldn't do without foreign investment to a larger scale because we needed capital, technology and markets. These are the determining

---

[6] The NEP, or New Economic Policy, was created by Lenin in March 1921 to help the Bolshevik regime respond to economic and social crises caused by foreign imperialist interventions and the 1918–20 civil war. The NEP was a strategic retreat to preserve the revolution: it created a private agricultural market and permitted the peasants some freedom of trade; and it encouraged capitalist foreign investment in nationalized industries under strict government regulation. Regarded by the Bolsheviks as necessary for the survival of the new Soviet state, the NEP partially restored capitalism while maintaining state ownership in order to help build up the productive forces. Given Russia's difficulties and the absence of other socialist countries, Lenin foresaw a prolonged period of a mixed economy before the socialist sector could sufficiently expand.

factors. The opposite would be paralysis and stagnation for a very long time.

All this is costing us dear. I already told you that any loan we take out is very expensive, and we have to discuss everything in very difficult conditions and in the face of very strong resistance from the United States. But we have to do it; there's no alternative.

The only road possible

Some of our friends have advised us to say no, that we are doing this because it's a very good thing. We have to be honest. We have gone down this road basically because it was the only alternative for saving the revolution and saving the conquests of socialism.

We had to establish joint ventures in a relatively short time period. We had to accept foreign investment. We had to do what we did in respect to the decriminalization of convertible currency, and you can be sure that doing the last pained us greatly, very greatly. We are aware of the inequalities that it created, the privileges it created, but we had to do it and we did it.

José Luis [Rodríguez] explained that today we are virtually operating in two currencies, that the day will come when we'll be operating in only one currency. There's no need to rush because this day will come. We have to proceed with calmness and patience until only Cuban currency is in operation. We already have the convertible peso, so we are working in that direction. In the existing conditions we couldn't rule out these possibilities.

It really is a great privilege for those who have a family relative abroad who is able to send $500, $1,000, or whatever, to have this available when many humble workers in the sugarcane industry, in agriculture and in other places do not have that possibility. But we had to do it. We had to adopt measures of this kind, which I know trouble you. And we didn't take them as an opportunistic action, we took them as a revolutionary action, as we have explained to our people once and a hundred times.

Whatever income the country obtains via any of these routes is not to enrich any individual, nor is it to line anyone's pockets. It is for the people, right to the last cent, to buy foodstuffs and medicines, to buy fuel for electric power, to buy indispensable raw materials for production, so that the country can advance. And whatever the difficulties may be, the country will advance in an orderly fashion. And the people, whatever the sacrifices may be, understand that this was the correct road, that this was the revolutionary road; and, of course, without the blockade, there would have been a lot of investment in Cuba.

Look what has happened in China. Look what has happened in Vietnam. There's been a flood of investments. Here there's been a flood of interested people, but there has also been a tremendous barrier of opposition to investment in our country.

With the consent of the people

In fact, I believe that it is very important, crucially important, that we have done this, as always, with the consent of the people. It cannot be explained any other way. Everything that displeased us also displeased the people, who are very sensitive, ultra-sensitive to any inequality, any privilege, since the revolution educated them to think in this way. However, it also educated them in the idea that the nation has to be safeguarded, that the revolution has to be safeguarded, that the gains of socialism have to be safeguarded. Independence has to be preserved and our rights to a future have to be maintained. That is absolutely irrevocable, and it is really very encouraging for all of us to grasp the extent to which the people have shown their capacity to understand all this. Only a people with a political culture like the one we have in our country today would have been capable of understanding that, and would have been capable of struggling and resisting.

Are we by any chance fooling someone? No, we're absolutely not fooling anyone. What we can state is that all the land in this country is in the hands of Cuban campesinos and agricultural workers. What we can say is that every house, almost every factory, every hospital. . . . Not one hospital, not one single school has been privatized here, and the country owns the overwhelming majority of its wealth.

So, what were we to do? We had to choose. Before a factory remained shut down, deteriorated completely or was lost, if some capitalist entrepreneur appeared who was willing to become our business partner, it would have been absurd not to have accepted, not to have gone ahead. When the socialist camp collapsed, thousands of factories were without fuel, without electricity, without raw materials, without spare parts. If the opportunity arises, even if only half of this factory stays in our hands — and frequently we retain the factory intact, when the association is commercial in character — we have to take it. It's the rational thing to do, and it's beneficial for the people to do so.

We cannot let ourselves be guided by what pleases or displeases us. Our criterion has to be what is useful or not useful to the nation and the people at this highly decisive juncture in our country's history. If there are kilometers of beach that can be utilized and we lack the capital to build the hotels we need in those areas, if we can form some kind of joint venture or admit an investment, we'll do it.

The hotels existing in Cuba today are the property of Cuba, or of joint ventures, and there are not many of the latter. It's a fact that the work of our adversaries has influenced the number of joint venture hotels we have. However, in spite of everything, we have been able to build hotels in the special period.

During the special period, using our own resources, we have constructed important scientific research centers, another of the country's economic sectors, and every one of these scientific research centers is the property of the nation. The country will preserve everything that can be preserved, and we will negotiate anything that can be negotiated.

The entire banking system in the country is national property. As I already said, practically everything is in the hands of the nation. But if we have to introduce a specific amount of capitalism, we'll introduce it; we are introducing it, with all its inconveniences.

I'm going to say one thing here: it could come to the point where we have an investment which is 100 percent capitalist. If some capitalist has all the necessary capital, has the market, has the technology we lack, there can even be cases of a company based on 100 percent foreign capital. In such a case we would be left with the work force and the taxes payable. We would have to resign ourselves to this.

It is preferable that the factory should remain ours, completely ours. It's preferable that the country reaps all the income, and that ownership remains with the country. We have seen this already, when everything belonged to the country.

At best, 50 years, or 100 years, will have to go by, or however many years. But always, if the country can retain something, it must retain it; preserve something, it must preserve it. This is a basic principle; but we're not afraid, and we don't have a complex. I believe that we are doing what revolutionaries have to do at this moment. Anything else would be an absurdity, a dream, an impossibility.

Power is the key

The key, comrades and friends, the key to all this is power. Who holds power, the big landowners, the bourgeoisie, the wealthy? I mention the big landowners at this point because that's what we had before. There are no big landowners here now; the only landowners we have here are the cooperative workers and members of the Basic Units of Cooperative Production, etc.; they are the only ones. Together with the tens of thousands of small independent farmers.

Who holds the power? Is the power in the hands of the bourgeoisie, wielded by the bourgeoisie and for the bourgeoisie? Is the power in the hands of the capitalists, wielded by the capitalists and for the capitalists? The question of power is key.

I must say also that we are doing some of these things to have economic efficiency and to improve our socialism. Obviously, my friends, it's pretty difficult to socialize or collectivize shoe repairers, for example.

There was a time here when there was such a battle, when everything was nationalized. But within society, and this will always be the case, there are several tasks that are really more appropriately carried out by a self-employed individual or various self-employed individuals, rather than the state attempting to undertake them. We have come to this conclusion.

This is in connection with self-employed work, born of specific needs, and not just to create employment or promote additional sources of income for workers, although these are fundamental objectives in the current circumstances.

The question of employment

So, before returning to the earlier theme, I'm going to continue with the question of employment.

In the situation of several factories being without raw materials, or without a domestic or foreign market, a huge number of unemployed people would be the result. What would the theoreticians of neoliberalism have advised? Turn all these people out onto the street, close down those factories and condemn millions of people to hunger, without receiving a cent. We couldn't do that. And not one worker has been left abandoned. They continued to receive their wages, or a percentage of their wages when there was no work available for them. If there was a surplus in one workplace, we tried to relocate them elsewhere. We have jobs, but not everyone is prepared to do just any job. However, we maintained protection for the workers.

When our levels of production abruptly fell, and money continued to circulate and grow in quantity, this led to a very damaging phenomenon for us which could not be allowed to go on indefinitely. In the early stages we applied the principle that nobody should be left unprotected. As a consequence of this we began to swim in money. There were rivers of money in the streets, and we had to begin collecting this money, because although during these years the overwhelming majority of people worked, you could say, from a spirit of patriotism, in fact there's always a certain percentage who don't have the same attitude. So when there begins to be a surplus of money coming into the home, over and above need, to buy the products on the ration book, if there are two people working, one tends to give up his or her job. At best, the person might have been a teacher, a professor, a nurse, a skilled technician who was needed in the factory, or in the health services, in the schools, in the hospitals.

Let's suppose that a hospital begins to lose staff. Although 80 percent of the personnel continue to work there in a disciplined manner, 20 percent have no need of money, lack a strong spirit of sacrifice, understanding or conscience and begin to miss work.

When a hospital begins to be short of nurses, or technical staff, or cleaning workers, that hospital starts to have problems, and the situation is the same in schools or other public services. We confronted all those problems surrounded by those rivers of money, and we had to start collecting that money, applying a large-scale austerity policy, of saving money, reducing the deficit, reducing subsidies, because the situation had reached the point where anybody could get 150 pesos for one dollar.

We began to implement measures, but they were not edicts dictated from above. We had to increase the prices on nonessential products, we had to introduce taxes, to suspend some gratuities. All those measures were discussed in the National Assembly, and subsequently in discussions with all the country's workers, then once more in the National Assembly, then back again to be debated by workers, students, campesinos. In every single sector it was discussed once, twice, three times, up to a fourth time, explaining it all, and a group of measures was adopted, based on discussions with and the consensus of the people.

The measures were applied in various sectors and the results are palpable. In one year, approximately 2.7 billion pesos have been collected, from a total of over 11 billion. People who had left their jobs began to resurface and return to work in the hospitals, the schools and the public services. We had to create the need for money and a wage, otherwise the service sector and production sectors, all the sectors, would have gone into serious decline. What was important was the method used to collect the money, and the results are those I have just outlined to you.

There is something more. Today anyone with a dollar would find it difficult to get much more than 35 pesos for it. We could say that we are one of the few countries in the world whose national currency has gained in value, and we're beginning to benefit from the measures we've been implementing. These measures are stimulating the economy and we are really getting ready to confront the situation. In the name of whom? In the name of the people. For whom? For the people.

That is why I would like to return to the idea that I interrupted some moments ago. This is the key, because if the people have power, if the workers have power, not the rich, nor the millionaires, then policy can be made in favor of the people, while respecting the commitments made to specific foreign companies, respecting everyone and the interests of everyone, because we are not thinking of nationalizing anyone.

All our business deals have been decided through a contract which stipulates everything, the number of years and so on. But while the people have power, they have everything. The one thing that the people should never lose is power, not today, not tomorrow or the day after tomorrow, not in the year 2020, 2050 or 2100.

This key idea is linked to the question of democracy and participation. If we say: "Look, we are of the opinion that our political system is better than in any other part of the world," there are people who would smile to themselves, who would think it was a joke. They are so addicted to political toxins, like the heavy smoker who gets through four packs of cigarettes or 10 cigars a day, gets addicted to the nicotine, or others get addicted to heroin, cocaine, marijuana or any of those substances. They want to impose a historical system on us in the name of who knows what principle, because until the middle of this century the world was full of colonies, and at that time there was little talk in the West of human rights or representative democracy.

The world 50 years ago

I remember a map of the world from when I was a child: Britain's African possessions were highlighted in red, and those of France in another color. France and Britain covered almost the whole continent between them — my apologies to the ambassadors here, both of whom I esteem and respect. I am talking of the past, ambassadors, not the present — and I could see on the map that there was not one independent country. I don't recall any, only the Spanish, Belgian, Portuguese, French and British colors. I then looked at Asia, and it was the same; China had its own colors but everyone knows that it was a semi-colony.

We are all aware of what prevailed in the world 50 years ago, and it was after World War II that the liberation movement in the colonies began. We know what Latin America was, without exception, and I include us, "yes men" or "yes sir" as Robertico was saying this afternoon. The orders arrived and, in general, were respected and complied with without discussion. However, we had our own colors on the map. Afterwards, came the Cold War and all the demagogy over representative democracy and various theories which emerged from the fight against the revolution and socialism. Their allies, living under shocking regimes of terror, were, of course, excluded.

Now, I am not saying that our model can claim to be the best model for everybody. No, I wouldn't dream of saying that. I believe that our model or many of our experiences could be useful to certain countries. I also believe that every country should create its own model, and should have the right to create its own model, and that no one can come along, in the name of whatever, wanting to impose whatever model they like on any country. It is as if we were to send a message to the Queen of England stating that a republic should be established there, because if they don't we'll establish a blockade of Great Britain. Or to tell his Holiness, the Pope, that he should establish a house of representatives or a senate, or universal suffrage for all the priests in the world.

I have used these examples because they demonstrate how absurd it is that there are so many people telling us what we have to do. Well, we learned to say: "We'll do as we like, and that's that!" Sometimes, it's useless to be reasonable; they keep coming back with the same old tune, over and over again. What we say is that our model is right for us, it is as simple as that, and we are not defending our model. We are defending our right to have a model. Now, if they want to, we can make comparisons and that's that.

One of the tragedies of this hemisphere is that during its independence wars models were brought in from Europe and the United States. Here they didn't only bring us the model, but they even brought us the Capitol — I don't know if any of you have passed by there, it was based on the Washington Capitol building — and is now a scientific research center, because our National Assembly meets in the International Conference Center or here, not in that Capitol.

That Capitol has become a historic monument. We see it as one of the architectural jewels of Old Havana. It is even a source of hard currency. But it is now a science and technology center, a library; that building which was once full — with all respect to some exceptions — of thieves and bandits of all kinds now has many, many things.

Every day there is a scandal somewhere in the world: in Europe, Latin America, Asia. The political parties have robbed, have received millions, or have bought votes. The transnationals or big business have given that much, or so much. As a general rule, I would say to the world's most splendid representative democracies: "Let he who is free from sin cast the first stone."

Now, is there a single assembly within these splendid democracies that does not have just one millionaire, that does not have just one multimillionaire, that does not have a tremendous lobby from big business and the transnationals? Is there one assembly that has not spent one cent on elections, that has not collected funds in some way or another?

How can you be a representative without money? Is there one assembly in the world that can say that not one of its representatives — and we have over 500 of them — did not spend a cent on their election campaign? Is there one among those splendid representative democracies? I don't want to point the finger too much so as not to cause offense.

"It is the people who nominate"

In our country we have an Assembly with unique characteristics; in our country the party does not nominate [candidates] for election. Is there any country in the world whose parties don't nominate? Yes there is one, it is called Cuba. It is the people who nominate! The people! Let's say it is a type of Athenian democracy, aside from the fact that in Athens there were patricians and slaves. The patricians had all the rights and the slaves had none, nor did other categories of citizens. For every freeman there were at least two slaves; those with political rights were about 30 percent. A Greek democracy, then, without slaves and without citizens deprived of their civil rights.

It is the people who come together. Flesh and blood men and women meet in their constituencies and propose the slate for their constituency delegates. It is they who elect, and it is those delegates from the constituencies that are the members of the municipal assemblies, and they are the ones who elect the deputies to the National Assembly, it is not the party.

The National Assembly elects the government. The streets are not filled with posters and placards and all that filth that we see in other parts of the world every time there's an election campaign.

In our country the ruling principle is that the people nominate and the people elect. There are many countries called democracies where it's the parties that nominate [candidates] for election: they draw up a list, and it's already known from surveys that one, two or three from the list are going to be elected, and that's it. It is the parties that select, whereas in our country they do not intervene. We do not have a multi-party system, but a million-party system, because every one of this country's 11 million inhabitants has the right to stand and to elect. Nobody tells them: "Propose this one," "Propose that one," "Vote for this one," "Vote for that one"; here, everyone knows it by heart.

And how can the miracle that 97.1 percent of the population went to the polls be explained? What do we see throughout the rest of the world? No one else has such a figure. There is no fraud of any kind here, and it is the children, the Pioneers who look after the ballot boxes. Is there any country in the world that does not have a police officer or a soldier with a fixed bayonet guarding the ballot boxes to ensure that they are not stolen between one point and another, that the voting slips are not switched, that the votes are not changed, that nothing is tampered with? Here, even the foreign press are first in line at the polling stations when they are counting the votes.

Ah! And if a counterrevolutionary slogan should appear, a smile this wide — on the faces of some, not all — they are waiting to see how many blank votes appear, how many counterrevolutionary votes and so on. You should see them there. They go there, they are present, there's no restriction or controls at vote counting.

It's our system and the people turn out to vote. Why don't they turn out to vote in the United States? Only half go. The president is elected with 25 percent of the vote. What a splendid democracy! And from then on, they forget about the citizens; you can get them involved in a nuclear war without them even hearing about it. A U.S. citizen gets up in the morning, reads the paper and finds out that they are invading some country or another.

Ah! That's how it is, that's it, because the president goes around with a briefcase. Or rather the nuclear powers go around with briefcases. I remember asking myself in the days of the Cold War: "What if the moment of crisis caught someone on the toilet?" And if by chance he was attending to his marital duties on that day? Hey! The briefcase and the rapid response. Not even the Roman emperor had that power. A briefcase he uses to trigger off the missile launchers, because he gives the signal. That's a very representative democracy!

That's a miracle without any doubt, my friends. That's why nobody goes to vote, or believes in the elections, or the people, or in the politicians.

Throughout the world there is a crisis of confidence in the political parties, and there are many people who are standing as independents and get results. Now, could a humble farmer, teacher, university professor, without one cent in the bank, be a deputy or a senator, for example, in the United States? Could he or she? What a difference! Here our deputies do not have a single cent, nor do they need any money, and they have to obtain over 50 percent of the valid votes to be elected. So, the people have faith, and they vote.

The last elections were an example. In the middle of the special period, the number of people who voted and the way they voted was really impressive. Why should we change that? Why should we fragment the country into a thousand pieces? To whose advantage is it to fragment the country into a thousand pieces? That is what has happened in the former socialist bloc countries: 25 parties, 35 parties, 45 parties. It makes one want to say, well, that's not the concept of the multi-party system, it's a crazy party system. It's unbelievable.

"Our people cannot be underestimated"

So, why has Cuba resisted? Because of its socialist system, because of its political system. Those who predicted Cuba's collapse should take a look at what has happened over the last five years. The more Cuba resists the more it is respected, and Cuba is ready to win the respect of the whole world. We will not be ridiculed or be made fools of.

Among the qualities of this people are not only its joyful, humorous and rebel spirit, but also its acumen. The Cuban people are really an intelligent people; or it would be better to say a people whose intelligence has been cultivated, because there are many intelligent people in the world who have not had the opportunity to learn to read or write. It is a national characteristic that the people are clever, they think, they reflect. Our people cannot be underestimated.

This is our system. Why should they change it for us? I repeat, why should they change it for us? What we have to do is improve it, which is what we are doing and what we've done with the latest reforms of the Constitution.

Some people say: "No, you have to adopt transitional measures." We have already made the transition. We made the transition 36 years ago and all the changes that had to be made. A transition to what, toward capitalism? No, there will be no transition toward capitalism.

It was said here today that Cuba is neither a heaven nor a hell. So, let's say that it's purgatory, where they say that people go; and from where, with a little patience and the help of a few prayers and whatever else can be done for the poor souls in purgatory, they can move on to heaven.

They say that there is a way out of purgatory, but there's never any way out of hell. If we are in purgatory, we are not going back to hell. At least we have escaped from Satan, and are patiently waiting for the moment of reaching heaven. Isn't that the case, Robertico, isn't that better? That is more or less what was said in the final declaration: "It is not as good as they say, nor as bad as it's painted." I'm going to be honest: I think that we are far better than our enemies paint us and not quite as good as our friends say we are. In other words, I totally agree we're not so perfect.

In all honesty, I couldn't say that we have reached half way along the revolutionary road in this country, even after the work that has been done by our people; even after the resistance that we have put up over the last five years; even after having stood up to the great colossus to the North, in what has become a unipolar world; even after we were left on our own, that is to say, practically without the support of any other country. I think there is a great merit in that.

If you have a sense of history and I think the youth is sufficiently capable — and will be more than sufficiently capable — then history will have to accredit this great endeavor, the great page that our country is writing in history at this moment.

It won't be heaven, but they'll have to give you an Olympic medal. For you, not for us, because it depends on you, above all the new generation, to ensure that our revolution reaches where it has to go, to that heaven that we were talking about earlier; although I know that Robertico disagrees with that, because he's already said three times that perfection would be the most boring thing in the world, true? But to think that perfection exists, Robertico, is the most illusory thing in the world, because what is perfect today is no longer perfect tomorrow. Didn't that Greek philosopher say that nobody bathes twice in the same river? So today's perfection is tomorrow's imperfection. It's true, we should be modest, we should be humble, but we should not underestimate ourselves. That is what I believe, and I'm not speaking in defense of my part in this question — I am guilty of many things — or of errors that could have been made, I am defending you.

Dear comrades, respected friends:

You wanted me to speak, didn't you! I have spoken.

I join those who have expressed their deepest and most sincere gratitude for your presence. We truthfully feel honored, we feel happy and we feel encouraged.

We will now continue our fight with greater confidence than ever, knowing that there are so many good and honest people in the world who understand us, who wish us success, who want to help us, and to put a grain of sand here and there.

We won't forget this meeting; and we'll be ready, on the orders of the world's youth, if it's needed — as we said yesterday — to organize not an international but a world festival. This time some 1,200 to 1,300 of you have come; with 10,000 it will be a world event. We have the organizational ability to hold it in this country.

We have an excellent youth; you have met with them over the past few days. They have organized everything, really. They sought the help and cooperation of anyone who could provide it; but they were the ones who came up with the idea, and the ones who organized it.

If it's been a success, it is fair for us to recognize our heroic youth's organizational ability.

After what I have explained to you today, it comes as no surprise that I should also conclude by saying with great conviction:

Socialism or death!

Patria o muerte! [Homeland or death!]

Venceremos! [We will win!]

We'll see each other again!

Recollections of student days

Speech of September 4, 1995

In this speech, President Fidel Castro marks the commencement of the 1995–96 academic year and reflected on his 50 years as a revolutionary. The event was held in the Aula Magna (Great Hall) of the University of Havana, where he had attended law school and began his life as a revolutionary. The speech took place on September 4, 1995.

First of all, I must apologize for the Olympian heat in the Aula Magna tonight. During 35 years of revolution, nothing has been obtained in the way of fans or air conditioning or anything. I don't know if this is due to a lack of architects or of resources, or if the architecture does not allow it; but you have to invent something, because if it's true that there is global warming, and it seems as if it is true, I don't know how we can continue holding events in the university's Aula Magna.

You were generous enough to link the start of this school year with the coincidence that on this approximate date 50 years ago — perhaps a few days later — I began my university education.

A day such as this is a special privilege for me, even though it's been a rough day, even though the National Assembly has been in session all day, even though they made me tour the inferno of this law school, very well remodeled, without a single window open. Delio,[1] you have nothing to do with that, your field is history. And

---

[1] Professor Delio, who had taught Fidel at the University of Havana 50 years earlier and had contributed to his becoming a socialist, was present at the speech.

there were all those lights of the accompanying cameramen and photographers, which no doubt gives the idea that one has the energy needed to fulfill the delicate task you have given me of speaking to you at tonight's ceremony.

I called this a privilege, because how could I not consider it a privilege? It's one of those things you'd never imagine, that one day, 50 years on, in the midst of a revolution, even at a difficult moment for the revolution, amidst the special period, this meeting would take place. It is possible that many of your parents had not yet been born 50 years ago, so you could say that I am meeting with the grandchildren of that generation who entered the university in 1945. Not even a fertile imagination could have conceived of something like this.

Without a doubt, it was also a privilege to enter this university, because I learned a lot here, and because I learned what may have been some of the most important things in my life. Here I discovered the greatest ideas of our epoch and of our times. Here I became a revolutionary and a devotee of Martí. Here I became a socialist — initially a utopian socialist — thanks to the lectures of the professor we were referring to earlier, Delio, who gave classes in political economy (and it was capitalist political economy, so difficult to understand and yet so easy to expose in its irrationality and its absurd aspects). That's why I was initially a utopian socialist, although thanks also to my contacts with political literature, here in the university and at law school, I subsequently became a Marxist-Leninist.

I lived through difficult moments in this university, very difficult, so much so that it is purely by chance that I survived those university years. I engaged in very hard struggles, with all the necessary persistence and determination, until other years and other epochs arrived.

"My first political experience"

I have to say that when I entered the university, I knew very little about politics, very little. What did I know about politics at that time? What I most remember is that I had a brother, or a half-brother, running as a candidate with the Authentic Party, there in Oriente Province. I remember that at that moment there were 42 representatives for Oriente Province and each party fielded its candidates. I would probably have been about 14 years old and I was going around teaching people how to vote. I went around the huts and houses in Birán, teaching people how to vote for Pedro Emilio Castro. I don't remember his exact number on the voting slip, but I had to explain to those people, almost all of whom were illiterate, where to go, about the party and everything, and where they had to put their X.

But don't think that I was a revolutionary at the age of 14, or that I was political at that age and had made a particular political choice, only that he was my brother and had promised me a horse if he won in the elections. In reality, I had very little interest in that campaign — yes, yes, that was back in 1939. But he used to talk to me, he was kind enough to discuss things with me. Young people always like to be in touch with things, to be taken into account, and he gave me that task which I kept at until the day of the elections, but all my efforts came to nothing. The Rural Guards arrived and prevented everyone from voting.

Maybe I need to make some historical rectification as to the exact year — I think it was earlier. I'll have to remember which election that was. I may not even have been 14 years old when I did that political campaigning, and Pedro Emilio was the first alternate candidate among the representatives for that party. However, it would have been a matter of luck if one of the representatives had happened to die and Pedro Emilio entered the House of Representatives and kept his promise to buy me a horse. You can imagine — perhaps some of you can't, but those of you from the rural areas will be able to — what the promise he made to me signified. I believe it was an Arabian horse; he promised me everything in that campaign. It was my first political experience.

Those elections were decided by force, because in real terms the Authentic Party had an overwhelming majority. The soldiers arrived, set up two lines, those voting in favor of the government on one side and those against the government on the other; the former voted and the latter didn't. That happened in all the polling places, especially in the rural areas. That was how they held the elections and that was my first experience with elections.

I remember a great bitterness when I saw how they attacked the people there, mistreated them, assaulted them, and thus I witnessed my first great political farce, the first fraudulent elections I saw in my life.

Later, the same thing happened in the presidential elections, and in this way Batista gained the presidency of the republic in 1940. Batista really was the strongman, the abuser of authority. The military ruled; everything was at the service of the big companies, of the big estates, of the major interests. They received all the privileges, sinecures of every kind.

There was tremendous abuse in the rural areas. It's incredible that a situation like that could have been maintained for such a long period, by a few pairs of Rural Guards from that army created after the dissolution of the Liberation Army, with its U.S. uniforms, its U.S. machetes, its U.S. rifles and Texas horses. That army created terror in all the rural areas of our country, which explains the fatal situation of our campesinos and our agricultural workers, who went hungry and were unemployed most of the time.

Fidel's childhood

In my childhood, I had the opportunity of living among all those very poor families. We went around with and played with their children. I thought a lot about that much later. Throughout my life I have remembered what I saw as a child. Perhaps those images, those memories and impressions awoke in me a certain sympathy and solidarity toward those people.

Throughout my life, the special circumstances of the place where I was born and my parents' occupation led me to have to make decisions. You wouldn't believe me if I told you that I took my first decision when I was in first grade, when I had to persuade the family that was looking after me or putting me up in Santiago de Cuba to allow me to be a first grade boarder in the La Salle Academy, which I'd been attending as a day pupil. This is how I came to be a first grade boarder at the school.

In the fifth grade I had to make another decision, to leave that school, principally over issues of abuse by teachers, especially physical violence against my person, which also obliged me to use violence against a certain inspector. I don't want to mention names, because those things belong to the past. I had to rebel and physically fight when I was in fifth grade, in the first quarter of that year.

From there, I went to Dolores Academy. There things were a bit hard for me — there's no need to go into the history of all that. In spite of having reached a better school, I could more or less respond to the demands of that center. Once again I had been sent as a day student rather than a boarder, so that, a little later, I had to engage in a third battle to become a boarding student.

I went there in fifth grade, and I was there until the second year of high school — they had already increased the program from four years to five. Then I decided to leave there for the Belén Academy, which was the best Jesuit school in this country. The idea attracted me. I felt more suited to the Jesuit discipline and their behavior in general.

At that time I did a lot of sports activities. From early on I liked scaling mountains. Every time there were outings to El Cobre or similar places, I used to get lost trying to climb some of the mountains that I saw on the horizon; or if there were torrential downpours, to cross swollen rivers. I enjoyed all those adventures; it was a sport that I practiced. The teachers were tolerant. Sometimes I came back late, kept the bus waiting two hours, and they didn't create a big fuss on account of that.

So later, when I moved on to another academy, I was in the best physical shape to practice a lot of sports, especially mountain climbing. All that came from the Belén Academy.

Was I a good student? No, I was not a good student. I have to start by telling you that I can't present myself to this generation as a good student. I attended my classes, that's certainly true, as Professor Delio was telling you today — not without some displeasure on his part, because he would have liked me to have been a model student in everything. The teacher was in my classroom over here, and I would have my mind elsewhere. I was explaining that I'd be sitting there with all the rest, the teacher would be explaining a subject, and I would be thinking about who knows what, or about mountains, or sports, or whatever else boys and girls think about.

Subsequently, I became a last-minute crammer, which is the worst recommendation you could give to anyone. Well, I was a good finalist. In that, I think I could perhaps compete with Ana Fidelia in that recent race when she won the world championship,[2] because the other students were ahead of me, and at the last minute I devoted all my time to studying: during recreation, lunch, dinner, as a self-taught student.

I was telling the professor that I studied mathematics, physics and science by myself as the end of the course approached, and that, in the end, I obtained good grades, way above the top students of the year. That was my last-minute effort. The Jesuit teachers really praised my efforts in this championship period; they forgave me for everything and judged me at the end of the course, when they wrote to my house saying they predicted I would surely fail.

I will never forget one teacher with a very strong character. He was an inspector who called me up one time, having gotten in touch with a man who was a guardian for me there, or a representative of my father, and told him that I was failing the course. I'm not sure if it was the second year out of the three years I spent there. He made his complaints. I studied as I'd always done and I remember one day when I was leaving the dining room the same severe inspector said to me, with a Spaniard's accent: "Do you know what grade you got in physics?"

Because I thought that there was something behind this question, even though I knew that I'd done well on the test, I acted the fool and replied: "No." He said, "One hundred!" The top pupil had gotten 90, the school genius had gotten 90 when he had to take the institute examinations, or the institute professors came to the school for the examination.

There was also a subject, Cuban geography, in which of all the students only one got 90, and I had that honor; everyone else got less. There was a great controversy between the school and the institute, about the books and the texts. And what book did Castro study from? What did Castro do? I studied from the same books as everyone else, but I also added things from my imagination. Now, I didn't invent any capes or bays or rivers, but I always added something of

---

[2] Cuban track star Ana Fidelia Quirot won first place in the 800 meter event in the 1995 Track and Field Championship in Göteborg, Sweden, on August 13, and is an Olympic medallist. In January 1993, she was almost fatally burned in her home in Havana, but, miraculously, she returned to championship competition within the year.

my own to the test, and for some reason he liked the test and gave me a grade of 90. But I recommend to you that you never leave all the studying to the end as I did.

No one ever managed to inculcate in me the habit of studying every day, and the fact is that they tolerated everything I did because of the sports medals. They treated me better than the Cuban national team. They didn't criticize me until the end. They never really taught me how to study every day.

As I said, the school was run by Jesuits, Spaniards. The Spanish Republic had ended two or three years before and one of the teachers or aides who was a good friend of mine told me about the executions after the war. He was there as a medic and told me long stories about the number of prisoners who were executed in Spain when the civil war ended. It made me very indignant. He told me about it as if it were the most natural thing in the world. He didn't make any criticisms of it, but the story he told was quite dramatic, considering everything that occurred.

Logically, the political viewpoint was conservative, right-wing. Technically the school was a good one in many things, but all the teaching was dogmatic. We mustn't forget that everyone had to go to mass and study sacred history. Delio, sacred history would probably be the only thing in which I could compete with you, because we had to study it every year, in the first and second year. Really, the whole time we were receiving a dogmatic education; the teaching was absolutely dogmatic. In general, there were some laboratories, some research, some things, but I think that that system of education needed to be revolutionized, because it didn't really teach the students how to think. We had to believe things even if we didn't really understand them. Not to believe was a sin worthy of hell.

This I say without any interest in being critical. I really don't have any desire to criticize that school, but I'm explaining the type of education they gave us, which was very distant from what is considered an ideal education for any young person.

Otherwise, life was good for me at the school because of sports, explorations, excursions, all those things. I had good relations with all the boys, excellent relations. I could be sure of that the day I finished the school year, because of the way they cheered at the moment when they presented me with my high school diploma from that school.

I myself didn't realize that I had that many friends in the school. I think it was because of the kind of relationships I had with everyone, without politicking or anything like that. But when I got to the university, what could I have known about politics?

What had I brought from that school, what had I brought from my home, what had I brought into the university? A profound sense of justice, a certain ethic which is acquired. That ethic must have Christian precepts, which I learned fighting injustices from a very early age, with a sense of equality in my relationships with everyone from an early age, and undoubtedly because of a rebellious temperament of character, however you want to describe it. I reacted; I never resigned myself to abuse and the imposition of things by force.

Batista comes to power

When I enrolled in this university at the end of 1945, we were living through one of the worst epochs of the history of our country, and also one of the most deceptive. I was actually living through the leftovers of a frustrated revolution, the revolution of 1933, which really was a revolution, because the struggle against Machado[3] turned into a revolution.

Someone mentioned that today, September 4, is an ill-fated date, because that is when Batista[4] came to power. No, the 4th of September was not ill-fated; the 4th of September is a revolutionary date. Today, we don't have to be ashamed to be starting the school year on this date because the sergeants simply rose up against all those compromised leaders. There were many revolutionaries in that

---

[3] General Gerardo Machado Morales became president of Cuba in May 1925. Though espousing nationalism, he was known to the U.S. business community as a friend. In 1928, by controlling the election process, he was reelected. During a period of increasing insurrections, his police became notorious for torture and killing. Five years later, faced with a general strike and the defection of his own military, he fled the country and went to live in the U.S. The 1933 revolution began less than a month later with the "Sergeants' Revolt" on September 5, 1933.

[4] Batista first gained power as a result of leading the "Sergeants' Revolt" in September 1933 against the U.S.-mandated presidency of Carlos Manuel de Céspedes, which was opposed by the military, militant students and revolutionary groups.

movement, and students even participated in that government, which removed all the old army guard from power. That is to say, Batista began his life with an activity that was revolutionary. The problems came later, when the United States started interfering. They butted into the internal politics of Cuba and made Batista an instrument for their interests in this country. At first there was a government, a pentarchy, which was later led by Grau San Martín,[5] a university physiology professor who had gotten along very well with the students. Then they named a cabinet with Guiteras[6] in a very important position, and a series of revolutionary measures were adopted by that government, which only lasted three months. The measures were worker-oriented, dealing with, for example, the electric company. I think this is when the electric company nationalization occurred, something which was talked about for a great deal of time after. A revolutionary government was formed which started to apply a series of laws until the United States toppled that government, and that's when Batista's behind-the-throne role began. That is to say, he kept on removing and replacing different governments and maintained power for 11 years, until 1944.

They committed abuses of all kinds, crimes of all kinds, thefts of all kinds. No one knows how much those people stole, how much they extracted from this country! He was the puppet of the United States.

Later that revolution was frustrated. Then came the big struggles. There was the strike of March 1935, an attempt to overthrow the government, which was repressed mercilessly by Batista's government. They sowed terror in the city and all of the country and

---

[5] After the "Sergeants' Revolt," a junta, which included Ramón Grau San Martín, ran the country for five days, after which Grau was named president by the rebels. The U.S., however, refused to recognize the government and pressured Batista to desert the rebels; supported by the U.S. Embassy, Batista overthrew Grau on January 15, 1934.

[6] Antonio Guiteras was one of the leaders of the 1933 revolution and a fervent anti-imperialist. As part of the provisional government, he issued many anti-imperialist decrees and nationalist and social reform measures, including the eight-hour day and minimum-wage laws. Following the January 1934 coup, Batista carried out fierce repression in which thousands of revolutionaries were murdered, including Guiteras.

frustrated the revolution. It's hard to determine the aftereffects of a frustrated revolution, although the political process followed.

Then came a complicated international situation: the rise of fascism, with Hitler acquiring tremendous power in Europe and arming himself to the hilt. At the same time, the Soviet Union was following a purge policy with all kinds of abuses and crimes taking place. Of course, all these things came out later, after Khrushchev's denunciations in the 1950s, after Stalin died. They practically decapitated the party and the armed forces. They decapitated everything and helped create the most adverse conditions when the war started, with the exception of the great industrialization effort.

Creation of the broad front

But at that time the Communist International, the Comintern, was also operative, and that was what outlined the policies of all the Communist Parties in the world. That was when they launched the slogan of a broad front; given the danger of fascism, a policy that all the Communist Parties followed with great discipline, we could say with exemplary discipline, creating a new situation.

Batista also started to call himself antifascist and he agreed with the creation of this broad front. The Communist Party had a very disciplined participation in this broad front policy, and I'm not making a historical judgment, far from it. Maybe it's up to the researchers and historians to consider whether under these circumstances, another variation, another alternative, was possible. But it was an unquestionably correct policy on the outside, because what allowed Hitler to come to power in Germany was the division among the German left, between the Social Democrats and the German Communist Party, which left the doors wide open for Hitler to do what he did later. In other words, perhaps an anti-Hitler policy should have begun to develop before, but in Cuba, a Marxist-Leninist party had to become allied with the bloody, repressive and corrupt government of Batista.

I say this because it has subsequent consequences, in my judgment, in the policy of the country. While the army repressed the peasants, the workers and the students, the party still saw itself as being obliged, because of international commitments, to become allied to that government; even though it must be said, really, that it was tireless in its defense of the workers' interests. All of the strikes, all of the fundamental battles that were carried out in that period for better wages, to improve the living conditions of the population, were actually carried out by the Communist Party and the working class Communist leaders with great loyalty, with complete dedication. But a large part of the people were anti-Batista, a large part of the people repudiated the abuses, crimes and corruption. And that contradiction logically brought many young people, people with revolutionary tendencies and people on the left to stop looking favorably upon the Cuban Marxist-Leninist party. This is the objective historical reality.

The war finished, and after the war against fascism began the Cold War, the United States' fight against socialism. The United States emerged from the world war with enormous power, much more wealth, with almost all of the world's gold hoarded away.

Around this time there was a change in the Cuban government: Batista lost the 1944 elections and Grau stepped into office. Many people were deluded into thinking that a government of the people, an honest, almost revolutionary government, you could say, had finally arrived. But that administration had already been subject to political erosion, politicking and corruption.

One of the biggest frustrations of our country was what occurred a few months after the Grau administration came to power. Of course, in those days everyone was calling themselves a revolutionary, everyone who had been against Machado, everyone who was present for the revolution of 1933, those who had been involved in that political strike, or the other one, and all the struggles over many years. They called themselves revolutionaries then and they had the government in their hands. Well, the politicians had the government, but there were many people who came from that group who called themselves revolutionaries.

Entering university and politics
At this time, I enrolled in the university, one year after Grau's victory. The protests about dirty business and misappropriations had already begun. Of course, the university was bubbling. Many of those who were with that government had been in the Revolution-

ary Directorate.[7] They were ministers. There was a great deal of confusion.

When I got to the university I was really ignorant, and I must have seemed strange to the Communists, because they'd say: "Here's the son of a landowner and a graduate of the Belén Academy — he should be a hard-core right-winger." I was almost something frightening for the few Communists in the university. There were only a few very good, very active real fighters, but they had to struggle under unfavorable conditions.

The repression had already started to turn against them too, because along with the Cold War came the repression of Communists. They started to marginalize them. There was a ferocious anticommunist campaign and propaganda in all the media, the radio, the newspapers — there was no television at that time — battering on communism from every direction. Many of its most capable and self-sacrificing working-class leaders were later assassinated.

The anti-imperialist sentiment had grown much weaker, and in our university, which had been the bastion of anti-imperialism — from the days of Mella,[8] to the epoch of Villena,[9] the times of the Directorate, the days of fighting against Batista — this anti-imperialist sentiment had already disappeared. I was a witness to all this. I talked with all kinds of people, law students, people in every major, and almost never heard anyone say anything anti-imperialist.

The university had become Grau's baby bastion. The authorities, all the national organizations of the police, the secret police, the

---

[7] The Revolutionary Directorate evolved out of the University of Havana in 1955. The Directorate collaborated with the July 26 Movement and the Popular Socialist (Communist) Party in the revolutionary struggle. In 1961 the Directorate, the July 26 Movement and the PSP unified as the Integrated Revolutionary Organizations (ORI), which in 1965 became the Communist Party of Cuba (PCC).

[8] Julio Antonio Mella founded the Federation of University Students (FEU) in 1923 and the Communist Party in Cuba in 1925. Under General Machado's dictatorial presidency, Mella was imprisoned and led a hunger strike. Later freed, he went into exile in Mexico, where he was killed by an assassin hired by the Batista dictatorship.

[9] Rubén Martínez Villena was a nationalist and anti-imperialist; together with Mella, Guiteras and Chibás (leader of the Orthodox Party), he struggled against Machado and Batista and established the revolutionary government of 1933–34.

bureau investigating enemy activities — I don't remember exactly what it was called — the national police, all these institutions were in Grau's hands. The army was a separate case, used for major repression of big strikes and such. But the police were in charge of those activities. There was a university police force totally controlled by them.

I practiced sports my first few months in the university, because I wanted to continue with this, and I also became interested in politics. But it wasn't anything concerned with the world outside the university, just internal university politics.

I nominated myself as a candidate for anthropology delegate. This was a special subject because it was material in which the students could be helped in different ways, with information about the practicals, with advisories about lab days and exams, because there were many students who didn't come to the university. They were registered but didn't attend classes. And I also organized the first-year candidacy. Naturally, there were second- and third-year students already trying to sway us over so they'd have the majority, because in the elections the delegates from different subjects in the same year elected the delegate of that year, and the delegates elected the president of the law school. That's how it was.

I started in these activities during my first year, when I was also playing sports. Before long, I could see that I wouldn't be able to do both at the same time. Naturally, I dedicated myself totally to the political activities, organizing the candidacy, supporting it, looking for support from other students. We worked well. We had to deal with some real slick politicos, but our work methods gave results.

I remember that on election day around 200 students went to vote. I pulled in 181 votes and my opponent got 33, and our party won in every subject and all the delegates of the first year. How was it in the final election? It was a united vote; the majority won and they elected me the class delegate. Somewhere around that time they also elected me school treasurer. To tell you the truth, this was strange because the law school didn't have a single cent, so it would be a very honorable position, the treasurer of nothing. That's how it started, in my first year.

Relatively speaking, I had already started to stand out. They started to notice me, and already, at the same time, the credibility of the government had begun to deteriorate quickly and we students protested against that government.

The Chibás rebellion with the Orthodox Party followers happened almost at the same time, which terminated with a party called the Party of the Orthodox Cuban People, in response to the frustration with Grau's government.[10] And we were already protesting against that government. The university leaders at that time had high government positions, cushy jobs and everything; they had all the resources of the government.

So my struggle got harder the second year when the law school became decisive in the Federation of University Students [FEU] election. So I did the same work the second year — the year that came after, the first year of the program — I continued working on the second and the first at the same time, and we used the same policies. But it must be said that the adversaries couldn't get a candidacy together in the second-year class. They just couldn't find anyone to organize it, that's the truth. And with the first-year students, with a similar way of working, we had another landslide victory. We already had two classes, and the government interests took it upon themselves to maintain the FEU in every way, and to want to win us over first of all and later to intimidate us.

In the law school, in that second year, in that second election, my opponents in the school were strong, and not all of them were pro-government. Because of this there was a certain division in the ranks. The result could have been otherwise; but one of those individuals, in the fourth year, as there were five years with each one having one vote, became decisive, and he was elected president of the school, even though he was weak, with the commitment to vote against the government's candidate in the FEU. I think I was acting a little precipitously and with great passion within the school's internal struggle, because with a little more experience I would have looked for some kind of formula for the election of someone more capable and loyal within the internal opponents, who still were not

---

[10] The Party of the Cuban People, also called the Orthodox Party, was founded in 1947 by Eduardo Chibás, a progressive leader of the reformist movement. Also a leader of the revolutionary movement in 1933, Chibás was well-known and highly respected for his campaigns against theft, corruption and cynicism in government.

very defined in one position or another, but who were not necessarily pro-government either. So the lower and higher years were divided, and the division promoted an individual who was seriously committed to vote against the government candidate in the FEU. This is the one who didn't fulfill the commitment to vote in the FEU for those who were against the government, so we took it upon ourselves to remove him from office. We simply got together a majority of four and pulled him out, because the delegates from the first, second, third and fifth years were all in agreement on the FEU candidacy.

That is how the law school became a bone of contention and the decisive vote in the university.

It must be said that at that time, and as a consequence of a frustrated revolution — as I was explaining before — there were a series of factions in the country that called themselves revolutionary, to which all of the media gave big coverage, and they were generally accepted by an important segment of public opinion, all of them for some previous event, because they had done this or that. So a series of revolutionary groups ensued. All of them, of course, were tied to the government, although not without rivalry among themselves.

So I was all alone at the university, absolutely alone, when, suddenly, in that university electoral process, I was faced with that whole mafia that dominated the university. They were bent on impeding the loss of the university at all costs. They controlled, as I said, the rector's office, the university police, the city police, everything, and they decided that it wasn't valid to remove the law students' president from office, with the simplistic argument that there was nothing said about removal from office in the statutes, in spite of the fact that there were important antecedents involving the removal of their adversaries that had been accepted by these same authorities. The rector's office invalidated the removal from office of the law school president. And therefore this was the vote that decided if the university would continue being in the hands of the people who supported, or in the hands of the people who were against, the government. That's the story.

All of that translated into great danger for me, because the environment that I observed in the university, ever since my first year — even though it was bearable, no one cared about us — was a milieu of force, fear and guns. And this group that dominated the university was closely linked to the government. They had all the support, resources and arms of the government.

In what sense do I think that I jumped the gun? Perhaps I should have prolonged that struggle and confrontation a little longer. Nevertheless, I couldn't resist the attempts at intimidation and threats, and I entered into open combat with those forces, open combat, alone. It must be said that I was alone, because I didn't have anything, no organization to take them on, no party to support me. It was a rebellion against their attempt to subjugate the university and forcefully impose themselves upon it.

Articles have been written about my university years. People have looked for materials, dates, everything. I'm not really satisfied with the articles, but I respect their right to publish them, and they are good enough. They have a lot of information, but there is a lot omitted, in general, about the situation.

Fidel is barred from the university

I'm not going to try to give a detailed account on all this, but I do know that the physical pressures on me were very strong, as were the threats. The FEU elections were approaching and it was the time when that mafia forbade me from attending the university. I couldn't return to the university anymore.

I believe that Luisito Báez Delgado wrote an article saying that I went off to a beach in order to decide on whether or not to return, and that I finally did. And I haven't said whether or not I returned armed.

I've told this story to my friends several times. Not only did I go to the beach to think, but I also cried at the age of 20. But not because I had been forbidden to return to the university, but because, in any case, I was going to return. There was a whole gang of them there — I don't know how many — with the authorities behind them. They had everything. So I decided to return and I returned armed. One could say that it was the beginning of my own personal armed struggle, because at that time armed struggle was almost impossible. I asked an older friend with an anti-Machado and anti-Batista background to acquire me a pistol, and he got me a 15-shot Browning. I felt extremely well-armed with the 15-shot Browning because, in general, I was a good shot. This was because I had lived in the countryside and had gained a lot of experience with the rifles we had at home, without anyone's permission, and with the revolvers and all types of weapons. It just happened that I became a good shot.

So why did I cry? I cried because I felt that I would have to sacrifice myself in any case, because after the fight which I engaged in at the university with the support of the university students, with the support of the school, with great support — and I'm referring to all those students in my year and the younger class, although there were also students from other schools taking part — I had to face the challenge of being banned from the university. I made the decision and got myself a weapon. It pained me a lot to think that perhaps no one would recognize the merit of such a death, that our very enemies would be those who would write the version of what happened here. But I had made the decision to come. Not only that, but also to put up a good fight. We didn't know how many adversaries there were who would have to pay for the confrontation along with me. I decided to return. I had no doubts about what I had to do.

What prevented me from dying that day? The truth was that this friend had other friends, and there were various people, various organizations and lots of people armed everywhere — some were young, highly esteemed, courageous young men — and he took the initiative. This friend had very good relations with the students and said to me, "You cannot sacrifice yourself like this." And he persuaded another seven or eight to come with me, people whom I did not know. I met them for the first time that day. They were excellent. I have known men, fighters, but these were sound, valiant young men. So I did not come alone.

Today I was asking about the two small staircases. We met up there beside what was the cafeteria — they would still have one, even in another place, because there's absolutely nothing in that area. The bullies and the mafia had gathered there, around and within the school of law. So I said to the others: "You three go in at the front. Three of us will go up the staircase over there. Another three will approach from here." So we arrived there suddenly and the people there, about 15 to 20 of them, began to tremble. It had never crossed our minds that we could put up such a challenge, power or force. But on that occasion nothing happened, they just trembled. I went to the university and continued going to the university, but I came back alone. That was one day. Then I came back again.

I was sometimes armed, but then another problem sprang up in that confrontation. They had the university police, the street police, all the repressive organizations that I have already mentioned. They had the courts, and Urgency Court, and there was a law stipulating that if you had a weapon, you went to prison. So I found myself in the third dilemma: having to face up to that mafia without being able to use arms, because if I did so, they would seize me and put me into prison. Those courts were very harsh, and one could be locked up on the slightest exhortation from the government. So I had to continue my fight against that armed band, almost always unarmed, because it was only in exceptional cases that I obtained a gun. Imagine, just one gun! But most of the time I was unarmed.

All that battle around the university and its position vis-à-vis the government had to be carried out, we could say, unarmed. That's why I say that it was an armed fight which took place in very peculiar circumstances, in which on many occasions all I had was myself. And they got tired of all that planning; chance and luck were very much the order of the day. On one occasion the whole anthropology class went with me to the place where I lived, surrounding me because I was unarmed, while the adversaries were organized and armed.

Those were the ups and downs of those times, because, in the end, the big battle for the FEU resolved itself. The whole situation was so tense that it was more or less resolved at the end of a meeting containing a mix of friends and enemies, and a candidate was sought who was neither from among our ranks nor from the ranks of those in favor of the government. There was a certain period of reconciliation and calm.

I'm giving a brief explanation of this because those conditions were so difficult for me. It was a relatively long period with many ups and downs and anecdotes, but with a degree of calm, and it was in the middle of all this that the Cayo Confites expedition arose.[11]

---

[11] Cayo Confites, a fey in northern Cuba, was the site of a camp in Oriente Province from which an armed expedition against the Dominican dictator Trujillo was planned in 1947. After a few months, the attack was called off and the expeditionary force never left Cuba. Its 1,500 Dominican and Cuban partici-

The end of the second year had already come. The fight was quite intense — yes, it was in 1945, 1946 and the middle of 1947. I had already been designated as president of the Dominican Pro-Democracy Committee as well as of the Committee for the Liberation of Puerto Rico. There was great opposition to Trujillo[12] at the university, and for things like the liberation of Puerto Rico. Albizu Campos[13] was around at that time and led in many of the uprisings, gave rise to many large demonstrations.

I haven't mentioned among all this, in the fight against the government, the endless amount of demonstrations that were organized to the Presidential Palace. In some of the photos that you see here and there, I'm standing at the wall of the Palace, making a speech against Grau. I'm there in front of his office. He wanted to talk to the representatives, but we did not want to have any contact with him. It was a protest against the killing of a student. I do not remember the exact circumstances; there were many other cases just like that one.

But while we were waging those hard battles which had their ups and downs, those people became increasingly powerful. It was the era of Alemán,[14] the infamous BAGA coalition and unbridled thievery. He had political ambitions. All those groups that dominated the university joined with Alemán. They used the noble Dominican cause as the flag for revolutionary politics.

It was around that time that the conditions were thought to be in place for the organization of the final onslaught on Trujillo, and

---

pants, of whom Fidel Castro was one, were imprisoned in Havana. Fidel Castro was one of the few who eluded arrest. After a hunger strike, all the prisoners were released.

[12] Rafael Trujillo Molina (1891–1961), a Dominican soldier, ran unopposed for president of the Dominican Republic in 1930 and controlled that country as dictator until he was assassinated in 1961. In 1946 he issued an amnesty to exiled communists, but when they returned he had them executed, after which the Cayo Confites expedition was planned.

[13] Pedro Albizu Campos was a Puerto Rican nationalist. He was leader of the Nationalist Party and of the Puerto Rican Independence Movement.

[14] Julián Alemán was Minister of Education in the government of Grau San Martín and engaged in flagrant corruption and graft, including misuse of education funds. He was a key target of the anti-Grau forces and was later murdered by the Batista dictatorship.

apart from the Dominicans themselves, many of these people were those who organized the Cayo Confites expedition, and Alemán, the Education Minister, supplied most of the funds. It was one of the most badly organized things I have ever seen in my life. They rounded up people from the streets of Havana, paying no heed to their level of education, political awareness and knowledge in general. They simply wanted to organize an artificial army as quickly as possible. They got together about 1,200 men.

Fidel joins the battle against Trujillo

I, naturally, seeing that the battle against Trujillo was about to be waged, being the president of the Dominican Pro-Democracy Committee, didn't think twice. I packed my bags, and without saying anything to anyone, went to Cayo Confites to enlist in that expedition.

But perhaps the most important factor in all of this was that I signed up alongside the vast majority of my enemies. I was curious: they respected me. If there was one thing I learned throughout all those years during which one had to look death in the face, unarmed on many occasions, nearly every day, it is that the enemy respects those who do not fear him; the enemy respects those who challenge him, and the action I took of doing my duty as a student won their respect. That's the way it was.

While I was there in Cayo Confites, at the final stage — because while Alemán had absolute control over the money, and was supplying all the resources for the expedition — Trujillo bought Genovevo Pérez, the head of the army, and that is when the conflicts between all those groups that called themselves revolutionary came to the surface. Many believed that they were revolutionary. They truly believed it, because what was a revolution? They did not know. Who could be the flagbearers of a revolution or express revolutionary ideas? The Communists, those who were defending the workers, those who had an ideology, those who had a revolutionary theory; and other than that, what could the revolutionary theory be? Many of them considered that the revolution consisted of punishing a thug from the Machado era or the Batista era who had committed crimes against the people. That was their idea of what being a revolutionary was about.

But all that began to deteriorate. It was also the time of the Orfila massacre. This group, which had the full weight of the police, repressive forces and all the rest behind them, were in a family home and shooting broke out. In their attempt to capture and kill one of the leaders of opposition groups, they killed even the lady of the house along with everyone else. The army was sent in to put an end to the battle that lasted four hours — we were in Cayo Confites.

A journalist who managed to take photos of the whole thing, which were published, rose to fame; it was a huge scandal. Genovevo, the head of the army, took advantage of the incident to call off the Dominican expedition, in which quite logically he also saw a political rival on the domestic front — people that would pose a threat to him should the rebel movement in the Dominican Republic have success. So they took advantage of the situation to wipe out any possible rivals. They imprisoned many of the top men, took away their power in the motorcycle police force, the Bureau of Enemy Activities, the judiciary, the secret and national police. They were removed from all the high places; they lost all their power.

Fidel first thinks about guerrilla warfare

So when the Dominican invasion was frustrated — and we were already on our way to the Dominican Republic with those who remained — there was much desertion, among other things. From that moment on I had the idea of guerrilla warfare. I had been given a company of soldiers. The whole thing was totally chaotic: no organization, no efficiency, no nothing. But I said to myself, we have to go. And I almost started guerrilla warfare in the Dominican Republic, because on the basis of Cuban experiences and many other things, which would take too long to recount, and on the basis of my conviction that one could fight against the army, I was already thinking at that moment of the possibility of a guerrilla war in the mountains of the Dominican Republic. That was in 1947.

On my return I was not put in prison. I had not resigned myself to the idea of going to prison — that is also a long story. I got out of going to prison and had managed to hold on to some weapons which were later lost because a denunciation was made. Just when everyone in Havana thought that I had been swallowed up by the sharks of Nipe Bay, the dead man turned up on the steps of the university. No one could believe their eyes, because I had not made contact with anyone until I arrived in Havana.

The battle of Orfila had brought about a change in the situation. The intervention of the army, the disarming of the main group that dominated the university, had brought about optimal conditions, and I think it can be said that the support of the students was total.

But then I was faced with the following problem: since the expedition was around June or July and had been extended beyond September, I had to take exams in certain subjects in September. But when I arrived exam time was already over and I was faced with a choice — another dilemma: to enroll for the second year again as an official student, in order to continue with my work within the official institutions of the FEU, or to simply enroll for examinations. That was a very important decision, because one of the things I could not tolerate was eternal students and eternal leaders who enrolled time and time again. I had made strong criticism of that and could not do the same myself. So I said, however powerful the arguments may be, I will simply enroll for examinations only.

Having enrolled for exams only, I was faced with the contradiction of having many, very many supporters at the university but not being an official student, which meant that I could not run for posts within the organization. But I did not hesitate in making that decision, and I am satisfied with what I did at that time.

When I returned, the situation had improved considerably; it was safer and calmer. That was when I took on the task of trying to organize a Latin American students' conference in Colombia, which would coincide with the famous OAS meeting,[15] where they were going to pass I don't know how many reactionary resolutions. We managed to get some people together. I visited Venezuela and Panama, places of considerable activity. While I was working with the students in Colombia, I was put in touch with Gaitán, a leader of exceptional talent with great popular support, who unfortunately

---

[15] At a meeting in Bogotá, Colombia, March 30–May 2, 1948, the Ninth International Conference of American States approved the Charter of the Organization of American States (OAS), supported by the Truman administration. The charter went into effect in December 1951, and later became a means of U.S. control of Latin America and of opposition to Cuba, as well as the Soviet Union.

was assassinated on that April 9, just one hour before he was to meet with us for the second time. We were preparing to meet with him when the insurrection broke out in Bogotá.

That's what happened in Bogotá — it's also a very long story. I believe that Alape, a Colombian writer, accumulated quite a lot of information on all that took place.

That's a basic overview of what happened. Of course, there was much more. I'm simply summarizing to give you a basic idea of the situation in which we were working.

Revolutionary consciousness

The most important thing for me was my political training and my acquiring a revolutionary consciousness. I had traditional ideas concerning the war of independence, [José] Martí's thinking; I strongly supported Martí and his thinking. I had read virtually everything there was to read on the wars of independence, and I then became acquainted with economic concepts and the absurdities of capitalism and developed my own utopian way of thinking, which was utopian socialism, rather than scientific socialism. My thinking concerned the chaotic nature of things, how everything is disorganized, with overaffluence in some places and unemployment in others, an overabundance of food in some places and hunger in others. I was becoming aware of the chaotic nature of capitalist society and was coming to the conclusion that that type of economy, which they told us about and taught us about, was absurd.

That's why, when I first came across Marx's famous *Communist Manifesto*, it had a great impact on me. I was also aided by certain university texts, such as *La historia de la legislación obrera* [*History of labor legislation*], written by someone who later was not faithful to that history, but who wrote a good book; also the work of Roa and the various works on political ideas. In other words, I was able to get to the heart of the matter with the help of texts written by various professors. I was even aided by the Popular Socialist Party library, where I bought everything on credit, because I didn't have sufficient funds to pay outright. As a result, I gradually built up a complete Marxist-Leninist library of my own. It was my professors who provided me with the materials which I later began to read avidly.

The Orthodox Party was founded around that time, with me being part of it right from the beginning, before becoming a socialist. Later I became something like the left wing of the Orthodox Party.

So what was the key element in everything that happened later? My conviction was that the Communist Party was isolated and that with the prevailing conditions, at the height of the Cold War, and the vast amount of anti-communist prejudice at the time in Cuba, it was not possible to make a revolution based on the positions adopted by the Popular Socialist Party, even though it wanted to make a revolution. The United States and the reactionaries within the country had isolated this party sufficiently to prevent it absolutely from carrying out a revolution. That's when I began to think about the possible ways and means of carrying out a revolution.

Given the level of activity in the country at the time and the great gain in popularity of Chibás' movement among the masses, I saw myself as being part of a party with great popular support, attractive concepts in the struggle against vices and political corruption, and social ideas that were not totally revolutionary. Generally, except in the capital of the republic, the party was falling into the hands of large landowners, because when a popular party emerged, the provincial administrations soon fell into the hands of the landowners and the wealthy. That process was already going on within the Orthodox Party. It was due to this contradiction and the tragic death of its strong and militant founder that I formulated the concept of how a revolution should be undertaken in our country's conditions.

With Chibás' suicide, that party was left without a leader. We needed to win the elections under those conditions. As a result of the support gained after the death of Chibás, it was inevitable that the Orthodox Cuban People's Party won the elections.

Faced with the impossibility of a revolution by that means and the inevitability of it being rapidly thwarted, I prepared a plan for the future: to launch a revolutionary program and organize a people's uprising from within that government and from within Congress itself. From that time on, I already had the concept totally worked out. I had established all the ideas that are in *La historia me absolverá* [*History will absolve me*],[16] what should be the measures, how to institute them, what to do. That was the first revolutionary concept that I was able to draw up, let's say barely six years after having started university that September. One could say that it took me six years to acquire a revolutionary consciousness and draw up a revolutionary strategy.

The July 26 Movement is launched

All of that changed when the March 10 coup occurred,[17] since it cut short all of that process and forcibly established a military government. That was another challenge and it wasn't our plan to make the revolution on our own. We thought that an elemental sense of national interest, an elemental sense of patriotic honor would cause the opposition forces to come together to fight Batista, and we began to prepare for that time, to fight alongside the other forces in what we believed was an inevitable and essential event for our country, and we began to prepare the people here in the university. It was a secret operation; some 1,200 members of the July 26 Movement were trained in the University Martyrs' Room here.

All of the experience in Cayo Confites and all of those problems taught me a lot. Some of those experiences we had during the first months of the clandestine struggle taught us a great deal about how to work, and we came to train some 1,200 members before July 26, with the cooperation of a number of comrades from the FEU and the university.

I'm going to tell you something else — I've never said this before — I had to train the people of the July 26 Movement in secret in the university, because there was a great deal of jealousy among the students following the March 10 coup. There were people who believed that history would repeat itself and it would all stem from the university again, as it had in 1933, and it did in fact come from the

---

[16] *History will absolve me* was Fidel Castro's defense speech at his secret trial on October 16, 1953, after the July 26 attack on the Moncada Garrison. He later reconstituted the speech into a pamphlet while in the prison on the Isle of Pines. The pamphlet became the basic program of the revolutionary struggle, known as the Moncada Program.

[17] On March 10, 1952, Batista staged a coup, suspended the Constitution and became dictator of Cuba.

university, but it came about in another way. And so, I have to say with great bitterness that there was jealousy among some of the students. I had to work clandestinely.

What had happened, among other things? When the March 10 coup took place, the only people who had money, millions, resources of all kinds, were the members of the overthrown government, and they began to mobilize all of those resources to buy arms, and, of course, those people felt a great deal of hatred toward me. You only have to look at the charges I made in the *Alerta* newspaper in the weeks leading up to the March 10 coup, and which were given the crowning glory of the front page headlines in the paper with the largest circulation in the country at that time. That was in January, February of that year. They tried to blame me for the coup d'état, and that was without two other articles that I was preparing, which were worse still, bearing the rallying cry: "You don't have to go to Guatemala."

This all stemmed from the fact that Chibás committed suicide because he accused several politicians of having estates in Guatemala and he couldn't prove it. He was subjected to extraordinary pressure; he became desperate and killed himself. I said: You don't have to go to Guatemala, and I began to reveal all the property that those people had here and all of the dirty deals that they were involved in. My new profession as a lawyer came to good use to look in the property registries and at all the title deeds, all the documents which were presented as irrefutable proof and which caused a great impact.

Thus, those people even sought to blame me for the demoralization which had led to the coup d'état, a senseless, unfounded idea but a strong one, and I found myself with those people with tremendous hatred for me on one side, jealousy in the university — I have to say it. And so that no one is left with any uneasiness, there was never any hatred or jealousy on the part of José Antonio,[18] never; he was always a good comrade and a good friend. However, the prob-

---

[18] In Mexico in September 1956, José Antonio Echevarría, a leader of the Revolutionary Directorate, and Fidel Castro, on behalf of the July 26 Movement, signed the Mexico City Pact Agreement, unifying Cuban youth and the revolutionary forces against the Batista dictatorship. In the agreement they pledged their commitment to carry out the revolution, standing for a program of social justice, liberty and democracy.

lem was that there was a revolution, and it seemed that there were people who wanted to wrench the revolution away from the university. Those phenomena occurred, and those were the conditions in which we organized the July 26 Movement. It was only when we saw the enormous errors of those who could have boosted the rebellion with all of their resources, the divisions between parties and organizations, and the incapacity for action, when there was no other alternative, did we decide to initiate the armed struggle with the forces of the July 26 Movement.

I think I have taken quite enough advantage of your patience. However, since you brought me here and since the comrades from the FEU asked me a good many questions when they invited me a few days ago, I thought these things would interest you and I decided to tell you about them. It is very difficult to tell people about things that one has been involved in. I have tried to do so in the most impersonal way I can, although I had no other choice than to pass on some of the experiences I lived through. That is why I have always felt such fondness for the university, which is precisely where those struggles took place.

I believe that in any analysis of my own life, nothing had more merit for me than the merit of those years of struggle in the university.

We continued to be united to the university in all the preparations for the 26th of July. We took part in those demonstrations because we had strength, one could say; we had proof of that. There were a lot of organizations and there were a great many people who were in this one, in another, in another, the same people. We succeeded in forming an organization of 1,200 trained members. We used many legal channels.

I forgot to point out that all of the 26th of July was organized in absolute legality. We used the No. 109, Prado district [in Havana] office of the Orthodox Party. I met there with each one of the cells. We sent them here to train in the university and then to other places. It was an enormous task based, fundamentally, within the youth movement of the Orthodox Party which, as I said, had great influence at a grassroots level, a great deal of following among the young people, and some 90 percent of the comrades chosen came from the ranks of the youth movement of the Orthodox Party, without the youth leadership. Of course we managed to carry out this recruitment working from below. Thus, some regions gave a lot of people, very good people, such as Artemisa, and, in general, all of them.

The revolution begins

We could only use around 160 of those people for the attack on the Moncada Garrison; for each member we used at Moncada and in Bayamo, there were eight who could not take part. We were really able to make a good selection from the groups that had made it that far, but all in complete legality.

There are a lot of stories and a lot of interesting anecdotes of how it all was, all those months that passed from March 10, 1952, until July 26, 1953. Suffice it to tell you one fact: I covered some 50,000 kilometers in a little car I had, a Chevrolet 50-315. I had bought it on credit; they were always taking it away from me. It burned out two days before the Moncada attack. However, at that time we rented cars. We were working in a different way, as you would expect, fitting to the conditions.

There was one thing in our favor: Batista's police didn't pay us much attention, since they were watching the Authentic Party, the Triple A and all of those people who had hundreds and thousands of weapons, and they knew that we had no weapons, that we had no resources. It seemed like just a pastime. They didn't attach much importance to us, and that helped us to work within the law all of that time, apart from a few odd occasions in which we had to keep a low profile.

And if there is something that I still need to say, it is that although there were disputes and there were conflicts — here in this university — which I have mentioned, many of those who were our enemies here, and even some of those who wanted to kill me and were making plans to kill me, later joined the Movement in the revolution, above all in the Sierra Maestra, in the guerrilla war. So, many of those who were adversaries here, and strong adversaries at that, later joined the July 26 Movement and fought, and some of them died. So, you can see the paradoxes that are a part of life, and how certain times give way to others. They had confidence and they joined us.

I've always had a great deal of admiration for the comrades who did that, a great deal of respect. And perhaps if there is something that we can feel special satisfaction over on a day like today, it is the fact that, although when we came here 50 years ago we found a fragmented society, a fragmented university, where the anti-imperialist spirit had been forgotten, where one could almost count the few Communists there were on the fingers of one hand, we have such a different university here today, 50 years later.

You are the antithesis of all that we saw here. And they were enthusiastic young men and women; they rapidly mobilized for a demonstration. However, there was no political consciousness, there was no revolutionary consciousness. There were the restless, rebellious temperament of young people, the heroic traditions of the university — because it must be said here that when I arrived at this university, I was very rapidly imbued with the university traditions, from the events of November 27 for the execution of the students in 1871,[19] to the death of Trejo, the death of Mella, the history of Mella, of Martínez Villena, the history of those who died, although they were not Communists like Mella and Villena, all of that history, without going back to more distant times which were recalled here today, such as the presence of Céspedes, the presence of Ignacio Agramonte.[20]

That air of heroic tradition entered the university and could be felt, and it had its effect on many people. The atmosphere of this university, which is what it had, what we found here, the raw material we worked with, had a special effect on us.

The opportunity of the present

Thus, the comparison between the university of 50 years ago and the university of today is impressive. I am not going to talk in terms of figures, of data, of how many students we have, nor of how many departments, you know more than enough about that. There were

---

[19] On November 27, 1871, eight medical students were executed in Havana by the Spanish colonial regime.

[20] Ignacio Agramonte (1841–73) joined the revolution of 1868 and became secretary of the provisional government. He was killed in the battle of Jimaguayú, May 11, 1873, an event that caused many to remark that the "soul of the rebellion in Puerto Príncipe" had been slain.

three universities at that time — two or three, I don't know if the one in Santa Clara was there — in 1945 just one, that was this óne.

If we compare what university education means today, suffice it to say that the number of university professors is greater than the total number of teachers and professors in Cuba before the triumph of the revolution, to cite one piece of data. However, without depending on figures, all of what that has meant, the 530,000 graduates, the bastion of the revolution that the university has been, without mentioning that, it is enough to see the quality of the comrades that form part of our school of law and our university today, the atmosphere, the spirit.

One has to feel happy realizing that none of you will have to go through the ordeals that a student entering the university 50 years ago had to go through. That is why one day after the triumph, when I came to the university, I said, what I suffered in this university is of greater merit than all that I suffered in the Sierra Maestra, because that was really the case.

The fact that you have been able to be freed from all that, that you have a university as you have, professors like the ones you have, a consciousness as you have, a historic task like the one you have, what a great difference! You can draw up your programs, make your plans, take part in everything, do everything, decide everything, have the privilege of living through this time, I would say the most glorious time in the history of Cuba. The special period will go down in history as the most glorious time in the history of our country.

Today, we see a people working miracles, inconceivable things, in the most incredible conditions; this course that began two or three days ago, that electoral process that took place a few weeks ago, in such difficult conditions, which no other country in Latin America has gone through, confronting such a great power.

What I told you before, when compared to what is happening now, adds up to a special kind of fate or a kind of destiny in which it has always fallen to us to engage in very difficult struggles against very powerful enemies: the struggles here in the university against such powerful people, the struggles against Batista, the struggles against the United States, and the struggles against the United States in the age of hegemony, of unilateral domination of the world virtually by one great power. And there has been the spirit and the presence of mind to fight and to resist. That spirit is present in our people and that spirit is like a seed that cannot die.

Today we also see it in the other peoples. Little by little they are overcoming the blow, they are reacting, they are devising new forms of struggle, and they are making it increasingly more difficult for the United States to rule the world.

Perhaps they thought that they had it all sewn up for a thousand years; perhaps they dreamed of those ideas that Hitler held of the empire of the Reich lasting 1,000 years, faced by a world which is more difficult to rule all the time, in which more problems loom up all the time.

Now, 50 years later, we are all involved in the same struggle. But now, 50 years later, we can also say that we will come out victorious.

Who would have believed that we would be able to resist one month, two months, three months, after the terrible blow we suffered? Who would have believed that five years after the disappearance of the socialist bloc, a socialist, revolutionary Cuba would still be here, fighting, standing firm? Who would have been able to say that we would be doing the things that we are doing now? Who would have imagined it? And now the world is beginning to acknowledge it, not only our capacity for political resistance, but also our capacity for economic recovery. It is true that we will get through this ordeal and all of the ordeals there are to get through.

If the fundamentalists come to dominate not only the U.S. Congress, but also the White House, there may be eight, nine or 10 more years of blockade awaiting us. However, I am sure that there are fewer and fewer people who doubt whether the country can stand firm. We will stand firm!

I look at you today, your youthful faces, the age I was when I entered this university. What struggles remain ahead of you! What battles you have still to come! But what excellent condition you are in to face them: united, with the country behind you, with the party behind you, with the people behind you, with the government behind you.

And those deep bonds built up between us have made possible the incredible participation and unity between students and the revolution, and great care has to be taken of that. The enemy knows that.

What wouldn't they give to be able to separate the students from the revolution. What wouldn't they give to be able to separate the workers from the revolution, the people from the revolution; and they have plans, they have different versions. And what I can ask you on a day like today is that you keep being, more and more, invincible and unyielding bastions of the revolution, invincible bastions, bastions that never surrender and never falter.

And in the name of the heroes whom we have mentioned here today, Céspedes, Agramonte, Mella, Villena, José Antonio — to summarize them all — I ask this of you: that our country can say, we have written a page that had never been written before and we have obtained the support of the students never obtained before, from the Pioneers to the university students.

It is of great satisfaction to think that the dreams of all those we recall are now in our hands. We alone can make them solid, indestructible. We alone, you, the workers, the campesinos, the people, can work this miracle which we are working, can put up this heroic resistance which we are staging, can live this historic moment which we are living, without any special merit, without being any way a model. I began by telling you what a bad student I was. Now, that was so, but I never got a grade I didn't deserve; I never cribbed on certain questions; I studied all the subjects.

I have a little academic record in there — I don't know if it's much; I would have to look into the details a little — of the 47 subjects in which I was tested over a year or so. I enrolled for 20 without being an official student, and I sat down to study, in the midst of other activities, but mainly studying, and I passed 20 subjects in a year. I enrolled for 30 the next. It wasn't that I had a mania for registering for classes. I had to do it, because I wanted to get four degrees: law, diplomatic law, administrative law and then a doctorate in social sciences and public law. I only had three subjects left for the latter, which I already knew very well.

At that time I was thinking of taking a break in order to study and I wanted to study political economy, but I needed a scholarship. I had to pass those 50 subjects to get the scholarship, and I had managed it. However, at that time events in Cuba gathered momentum and I changed my plans. I gave up on those projects and devoted myself entirely to the revolutionary struggle.

Don't take me as a role model. I accept the honors that you have given me as an act of generosity, friendship and affection from all of you. I don't consider myself to be a role model, much less a model of a good student. I have tried to be a good revolutionary. I have tried to be a good soldier. And if it does occur to some of you to imitate a case like mine, I beg you to imitate my few successes and spare yourselves the many errors that I may have committed.

And so, with absolute, total and sincere modesty, I accept this act of affection with which you have honored me this night, and you have obliged me to take on that horrible task of having to talk about myself.

United Nations

Speech of October 21, 1995

President Fidel Castro, representing the Republic of Cuba, addressed the special session of the United Nations on the occasion of its 50th anniversary on October 21, 1995, in New York.

The United Nations was created half a century ago after a monstrous war during which, on average every year, in its most intense moments, 10 million lives were lost. Today, 20 million men, women and children die every year from hunger and curable diseases. People in the rich countries have a life expectancy of up to 80 years, other peoples barely 40 years. The lives of billions of people are curtailed. How long do we have to wait for this killing to cease?

The Cold War has ended, but the arms race continues and military and nuclear hegemony is being perpetuated. How long do we have to wait for the complete proscription of all weapons of mass destruction, for universal disarmament and the elimination of the use of force, arrogance and pressure in the context of international relations?

The anachronistic privilege of the veto and the abuse of the Security Council by the powerful nations enshrine a new form of colonialism within the United Nations. Latin America and Africa do not have one single permanent member on the Security Council. India, on the continent of Asia, with almost one billion inhabitants, does not share in this responsibility. How long do we have to wait before the democratization of the United Nations, the independence and sovereign equality of states, nonintervention in their internal affairs and genuine international cooperation are made a reality?

The prodigious advances in science and technology increase daily, but their benefits do not reach the majority of humanity, and fundamentally continue to be at the service of an irrational consumerism which squanders the earth's limited resources and is a grave threat to life on the planet. How long do we have to wait for rationality, equity and justice in the world?

Our forests are decreasing, the atmosphere is being poisoned and rivers polluted. Countless species of plants and animals are perishing. The soils are becoming impoverished. Old and new epidemics are spreading, while the world's population is growing, multiplying the legions of the dispossessed.

Will the coming generations reach the land promised 50 years ago? How many hundreds of millions have already died without contemplating it? How many have been the victims of oppression and plunder, of poverty, hunger and ill-health? How many more will still have to fall victim?

We want a world without hegemony, without nuclear arms, without racism, without nationalists and religious hatred, without outrages against the sovereignty of any country, and with respect for peoples' independence and free self-determination; a world without universal models which completely fail to consider the traditions and cultures of all the peoples that make up humanity, without cruel blockades which kill men, women and children, young people and old, like silent atom bombs.

We want a world of peace, justice and dignity, in which everybody, without any exception, has the right to well-being and to life.

Thank you very much.

Cuba and Vietnam

Speech of December 10, 1995

*President Fidel Castro spoke at a reception held in the Reunification Pal-
ace, Ho Chi Minh City, Vietnam, on December 10, 1995, during his second visit to Vietnam, after an absence of 22 years. He came to Vietnam
from China, where he met with President Jiang Zemin, Prime Minister
Li Peng and other Chinese leaders. During his stay in Vietnam, he met
with leaders in Hanoi, including Do Muoi, general secretary of the
Communist Party of Vietnam; President Le Duc Anh; Prime Minister
Vo Van Kiet; and former Prime Minister Pham Van Dong.*

Comrade Vo Tran Chi recalled the time I visited Vietnam 22
years ago. Those were very difficult times, very hard. I came
from the Nonaligned Conference in Algeria, and stopped
over in India; and it was there that we heard the bitter news of the
coup d'état in Chile, which resulted in the overthrow and death of
that great friend of progressive peoples throughout the world, and
that friend of Vietnam and of Cuba, Salvador Allende.

I had planned a program of extensive visits, which I was obliged
to reduce because of those events, but I did have the opportunity to
make a visit to the south.

I came in a little AN-26 aircraft. Throughout the journey, I saw
the signs of war: thousands upon thousands of bombs launched on
the Vietnamese people, aimed at communications and bridges. Every

bridgehead was riddled with holes, resulting from the attempt to destroy communications.[1]

We had to travel over many roads and cross improvised bridges to reach the McNamara line, along the 17th parallel,[2] and there our Vietnamese companions showed me the battlegrounds of a few months earlier, the major battles of Quang Tri and other sites.

I was really amazed to see how the Vietnamese combatants had managed to breach those extraordinary fortifications, full of trenches, cannons and steel-strengthened fortifications, which had to yield to the thrust and valor of the Vietnamese fighters.

They introduced me to many fighters and many heroes. I met with military units, and I remember a flag that was put in my hands, which I let fly there. Photographs still exist of that visit, very beautiful images, and the photos of the flag of a valiant people, which I keep as one of the greatest treasures of my life. But at that time, the country was still not unified; a large part of the south still remained to be liberated. More time was to pass; much work had to be undertaken in organizing and preparing for the final battle.[3]

---

[1] By the end of the Vietnam War, the United States had dropped seven million tons of bombs on Vietnam, more than double the amount dropped on Europe and Asia in World War II, leaving millions dead and more than 20 million bomb craters. In addition to the attacks on communication and transportation targets were unprecedented numbers of bombings of civilian targets, most of them in South Vietnam, in the futile effort to destroy the will of the Vietnamese people. See Howard Zinn, "The Impossible Victory: Vietnam," in *A People's History of the United States* (New York: HarperCollins, 1995).

[2] The 17th parallel was the arbitrary line dividing North and South Vietnam created by the Geneva Conference upon France's withdrawal in 1954. Following Vietnam's defeat of the French colonialists after more than 100 years of colonial rule and an eight-year war for independence, the Geneva accords temporarily divided Vietnam pending free elections. In 1956, when Ho Chi Minh's electoral victory was virtually assured, the corrupt, U.S.-installed premier of South Vietnam, Ngo Dinh Diem, cancelled national elections and declared South Vietnam independent, prompting the next phase of Vietnam's struggle — for unification and sovereignty. Robert McNamara, U.S. secretary of defense under Presidents Kennedy and Johnson (1961–68), was widely seen as the architect of the U.S. war against Vietnam. Because of his prominent role in conducting the war, the 17th parallel was sometimes referred to as the "McNamara line."

[3] In January 1973, the United States agreed to a ceasefire, leading to the withdrawal of U.S. troops over the following several months. The war to liberate the South from the U.S.-trained and -armed forces continued until the fall of Saigon,

Those were difficult times, complex times. The Vietnamese leadership, acting with great wisdom, had achieved the agreements which committed the United States to a troop withdrawal. Those troops had been overcome, and they were retreating, but a massive puppet army of one million men remained, armed to the teeth, with the best airplanes, the best tanks, the best U.S. arms.

However, I had absolutely no doubt that when those troops came up against the Vietnamese patriots they would not be able to resist for very long. Those were my feelings then, and I was sure of victory. For that reason, when the last battles were initiated some months later, and the world received the news of the liberation of this city — at that time called Saigon, and from then on named Ho Chi Minh City — the world celebrated that victory as one of the greatest events in modern history.

"The dreams of Ho Chi Minh were realized"
Along the way we talked with our Vietnamese companions. How much money did the United States spend here in South Vietnam? A trillion dollars in order to prevent Vietnamese reunification, independence and sovereignty. But one day those dreams of Ho Chi Minh were realized. He said that there was nothing more precious than independence and freedom, and that after the war you would build a Vietnam one thousand times more beautiful.

What an exceptional man! What a far-sighted vision! What a profound conviction! How prophetic! Within 15 years, Vietnam was unified. Fifteen years later, and although he was dead, that reunification, independence and sovereignty had been won, and now this great work of reshaping and reconstructing a Vietnam one thousand times more beautiful is in progress.[4]

---

later named Ho Chi Minh City, on April 30, 1975. The unified Socialist Republic of Vietnam was proclaimed in 1976.

[4] Ho Chi Minh (1890–1969) was the leader of Vietnam's national liberation movement against the Japanese, French and U.S. imperialists. In 1941, he organized an independence movement, the Viet Minh, against the Japanese occupation during World War II. Following the war, he led Vietnam's successful struggle against the restored French colonial government (1946–54); and as North Vietnam's first president (1954–69), he led until his death North Vietnam's fight against the United States and its South Vietnamese puppet governments to reunify Vietnam (1961–75). While living in France, Ho Chi Minh was a founding

Neither can we forget Ho Chi Minh's advice to the international communist movement: Unite! Keep yourselves united! How Ho Chi Minh would have suffered if he had witnessed the disappearance of the European socialist camp, if he had witnessed the disintegration of the Soviet Union! What a heavy blow, so terrible for the world and for all its peoples, such as Vietnam and Cuba!

But since just ideas are invincible, the countries that persisted in socialism were not brought down. They had the capacity to fight; they had the capacity to persist in socialism; and they were capable of resisting, as Vietnam has done, as Cuba has done, and as other countries close to Vietnam have done. For that reason I feel optimistic.

Those who applauded the disappearance of the European socialist bloc and the disappearance of the Soviet Union believed that was the end of socialism. It may be very far from the end of socialism and close to being the beginning of the end of capitalism. All those who believed that socialism was disappearing thought that capitalism could be eternal; and nothing can be eternal, much less capitalism, so full of contradictions and injustices.

The capitalists who applauded then are now shocked by what is happening in the former Soviet Union and by what is happening in the former European socialist countries. There are many people in those countries who vacillated, but who now are thinking, meditating. They see the disorder, lack of discipline and chaos, and they are perceiving that capitalism has no future. Only the countries that are persisting in socialism — in spite of the enormous difficulties resulting from our being left almost alone — using our intelligence, using our hearts, using our creative spirit, are capable of introducing innovations that will not only save socialism, but will improve it, and one day will bring it to a definitive triumph.

"The future is socialism"

Because of this, today, in these times, we can say: the future — and this can be said with more conviction than ever before — is one of socialism. Capitalism is in crisis; it does not have solutions to any of

---

member of the French Communist Party in 1920; he also founded and led the Viet Nam Communist Party (1930), which later became the Workers Party of Vietnam.

the world's problems. Only peoples such as those of Vietnam, Cuba and other countries, who did not abandon the principles of Marxism-Leninism, or of popular democratic government, or of the leadership of the Communist Party, are now forging ahead and achieving results not experienced by any other country in the world.

Cuba is in a special situation, being very close to the United States, 90 miles away. There is even a military base on our territory. And a rigorous and criminal blockade is still maintained against Cuba, because they cannot allow there to be socialism in the Caribbean, socialism in Latin America, socialism on the doorstep of the United States. They thought that we would also fall within a few days. But five years have gone by and we are still standing, firm, solid, with the great support of international opinion. And despite the great sacrifices we have to make, we have resisted, will continue to resist and are starting to move forward.

So others fell. In my view, they fell like a meringue. But our revolution was not made of egg white, and I am sure that the egg white with which some socialist countries fell will turn into iron, and that they will once again defend and uphold the just ideas that they used to defend. That will happen when consciousness is totally awakened, when they regret previous actions, when they see with all clarity those orderly countries, where everyone had clothes, food, medicine, education, and there was no crime, no mafia; when all those countries en masse realize the great historic mistake they made when they destroyed socialism. Then history will save a place of honor for those peoples who, under such difficult conditions, were able to maintain their socialist principles, and figuring among the ranks of those peoples, like inseparable twin brothers, will be Vietnam and Cuba.

Some moments ago, when this ceremony was being announced, the names of many people who wrote heroic pages of history were mentioned. It gave me great satisfaction to hear those names, because they symbolize the heroism of this people that lasted for decades, this people who shed so much blood while others did business with the blood of Vietnam, while others improved their economies at the expense of Vietnam's blood, while others progressed at the expense of Vietnam, which they thought had been defeated, which they thought had been destroyed.

Today, many of those countries recognize Vietnam, admire Vietnam, make peace with Vietnam and cooperate with Vietnam. And though noble Vietnamese blood was turned into gold and money for many, today Vietnam is growing more than any other country in the region. Today, the noble and generous blood of the Vietnamese is being converted into well-being, prosperity and happiness for the people.

I would like to embrace all those heroes present and mentioned here, with all my heart; from those who threw bombs at this building, or were imprisoned for many years, to the families and widows of the martyrs. The world has rarely seen so much honor, so much merit and so much glory.

For this reason, we Cubans who are here, who have been given such a warm welcome by you, feel full of joy, full of honor, and full of glory at having received your tribute, hospitality and fondness.

Long live just ideas, because they will never be defeated!

Long live independence and sovereignty, because there is nothing more beautiful, as Ho Chi Minh said!

Long live the Vietnam that is being constructed today, one hundred times more beautiful!

Long live the exploited of the world who will one day also build a more beautiful future!

Long live the friendship — not the friendship — long live the eternal sisterhood between the peoples of Vietnam and Cuba!

Bay of Pigs anniversary

Speech of April 16, 1996

President Fidel Castro gave this speech at the ceremony marking the 35th anniversary of the Bay of Pigs invasion,[1] held in Matanzas on April 16, 1996.

After a day of so many memories and so many emotions, of seeing so many lovely things, of so many marvelous words, it's difficult to talk here today. But it was indispensable for us to meet here, because a day like this one could not be overlooked.

We commemorate many things this afternoon, many important things. But in the first place, we should remember that on this date, in the afternoon, we proclaimed the socialist character of the revolution. We could say that it was the first great artillery salvo in response to the aggression.

This afternoon we recall with infinite pain how we buried the comrades who died in the repugnant and cowardly bombing on April 15, a bombing carried out by planes painted with the insignia of our air force, to confuse us, to deceive us, to surprise us.[2]

---

[1] On April 17, 1961, U.S.-backed mercenaries landed in Cuba at Playa Girón on the Bay of Pigs in the south of the island. The invasion force of 1,500 largely Cuban-born counterrevolutionaries was defeated within 72 hours.

[2] On April 15, 1961, B-26 bombers painted with Cuban air force insignia attacked Cuba. One of these planes was flown to Miami by Mario Zuñiga posing as a defector. The following day, at a mass funeral for the seven Cubans killed in the bombing raids, Fidel Castro for the first time defined the revolution's goals as socialist.

I recall the early morning of that day, because I had spent the whole night awake. A boat was approaching the eastern zone and the comrades from that region were on a state of alert, especially in the area between Maisí and Baracoa. From the command post in a house in Nuevo Vedado [a neighborhood in Havana], we saw the planes that were going to bomb Ciudad Libertad flying low overhead. They fired almost immediately, but I remember that no more than 20 seconds passed before our anti-aircraft artillery responded energetically to their fire, despite the fact that it was made up of young, inexperienced militiamen with no practice in the use of those weapons.

One of those planes — as part of a deliberate enemy plan — flew off to Miami, landed there and said that it was deserting from the Cuban Air Force and that the revolution's air force was up in arms. They said that these were not U.S. planes with Cuban insignia, but rather planes piloted by insurgents. That same lie was proclaimed at the United Nations, and not even that country's representative in the UN was told the truth about what had happened. He was a person known to have relatively decent attitudes and perhaps they were afraid that he would tell the truth if he knew it.

That's the way they do everything, and that's the way they have done everything throughout history in all their wars of aggression.

Those difficult days of the Bay of Pigs

Those days of the Bay of Pigs were difficult. We knew that the United States would not pardon us for making a revolution. What kind of a revolution was it? It was a revolution of justice. All those laws that were mentioned here were simply laws of justice, in a country that was enslaved, exploited, humiliated; where the peasants had no land; where the U.S. companies were the powerful owners of the country's best land; where theft was constant; where people were killed, tortured and assassinated; where the number of illiterates was enormous; where almost 60 children per 1,000 live births died every year; where there were no schools; where 10,000 teachers were out of work. It was a colony in which there lived a valiant, heroic people who had struggled a long time so that their powerful neighbor would not take them over. Agrarian reform laws and urban reform laws had been passed. In short, because of these social justice reforms that neighbor decided to immediately liquidate the revolution. First they thought they could liquidate it by taking away the sugar quota or eliminating the oil supplies — that is, not selling petroleum to Cuba or permitting any other country to sell Cuba petroleum — and other similar measures; but the revolution found ways to fight each one of these and to survive.

They were not going to allow our revolution to be an example for the peoples of Latin America living under similar conditions, and they disdainfully believed that they could crush us. They did not realize that this was a different kind of revolution, that this was a popular revolution, a revolution of the people, by the people and for the people which defeated one of the best organized and best trained armies in the hemisphere.

They did not understand that, and immediately they took on the task of organizing subversive groups. Relying on the large landowners, the henchmen and others affected by the revolution, they managed to organize 300 groups and supply them with arms, resources, money, political support and aid of all kinds. They began to carry out sabotage throughout the length and breadth of our national territory, in addition to the economic blockade aimed at starving us to death.

At that time, the socialist bloc existed — the Soviet Union existed. As proof of their feelings of solidarity and internationalism they helped us, they supported us, and although we disagree with most, if not all, of what they did later on, we are thankful for what they did for us at that time. It was extremely important.

We were not willing to renounce the revolution

We did not want to mix up the international situation and the Cold War with our revolution, but we were not willing to renounce our revolution. We did not buy our first weapons from the socialist bloc; we went to Western countries to buy weapons. In some places we bought rifles, grenade launchers, ammunition, modern and automatic rifles. In a European country we also bought cannons and munitions. And what happened? When the second ship [*La Coubre*] was landing, having been sabotaged while abroad, it exploded — twice, as it had been designed to do — and in a matter of seconds more than 100 workers and soldiers who were unloading the shipment were killed. While they were planning their aggression against Cuba, they wanted to impede our acquisition of arms. At that time we didn't even have diplomatic relations with the Soviets, but we were determined to defend ourselves, we were determined to fight, and that was how we acquired the first weapons from the socialist bloc. Of course, they came from different places: some were Czech, others were weapons taken from the Germans during World War II and others were Soviet arms that arrived through Czechoslovakia.

In a short time a great quantity of weapons arrived in Cuba. It's possible that thousands of ships have brought weapons to our country and there was never another one that exploded. We did all the tests possible; we even launched boxes of munitions, boxes of grenades from thousands of meters away, and not a single box or projectile exploded. So we concluded that the explosion could not have been an accident.

Weapons arrived, but the people were not trained in their use. We had learned how to handle a few cannons and tanks which had remained in Cuba when the revolution triumphed, and that's how we started to arm ourselves, but we had to organize the cadres. That was the importance of what [José Ramón] Fernández[3] was explaining, that we had to prepare thousands of cadres in a matter of weeks or months, because we didn't know how much time we had.

When the United States saw that the revolution was resisting, it speeded up its plans for the mercenary invasion. We knew — after all the measures that they had taken against Cuba, including subversion, sabotage and armed actions — that as soon as they had the opportunity or the organized force, they would strike, trying to do in Cuba something similar to what they had done in Guatemala in 1954. No one could know when or how, so in the meantime we organized ourselves feverishly throughout the country.

We sent the first FAL rifles that arrived to the mountains where we were already preparing to fight if an attack began; the concepts that we later developed on a large scale were already present. We already knew that if the U.S. army arrived here, the Cuban people,

---

[3] José Ramón Fernández, an officer in the Cuban army, was imprisoned for opposing the Batista dictatorship. After the 1959 revolution he directed the Militia Training Schools and led them at the 1961 Bay of Pigs invasion. For many years Minister of Education, he is now a Vice-President of the Council of Ministers.

with tens of thousands of rifles, could fight them off. No one doubted that. Later, a torrent as we could call it, of arms of all kinds arrived, arms of a different type — hundreds of anti-aircraft weapons, hundreds of artillery weapons, hundreds of tanks, or at least it seemed like hundreds to us. I couldn't say how many we had on April 17, 1961, but I can assure you we had enough to crush 10 Bay of Pigs invasions simultaneously, in a slightly longer time of course. When those arms arrived, the population was mobilized throughout the country and especially in Havana. Most of the arms were concentrated there because it was logical that any enemy attack would try to focus on the capital of the country. Tens of thousands of militia were mobilized.

There were a few Czech and Soviet instructors and when they saw how things were, they said, "This is impossible. They need at least two years to train all these people." And we told them, "No, we have to train them all, and as fast as possible." That's when we decided to ask the trainees to teach in the afternoon what they had learned in the morning about tanks, artillery, anti-aircraft weapons, whatever. And that's what they did. In the end, those small groups of instructors were convinced that in this way it was possible to train hundreds of thousands.

We recruited many young people in the universities, in workplaces, everywhere, for the artillery, anti-aircraft units and infantry battalions, while we accelerated the instruction of the Rebel Army troops that had come down from the Sierra Maestra or had been incorporated throughout the country. We prepared the personnel very quickly, because we could say that most of those armaments arrived just a few weeks, or at most a few months, before the Bay of Pigs invasion. As you know, Cubans learn quickly.

As for aircraft, they had left us some Sea Furies, other fighter jets whose name I don't recall at this moment, some B-26s and three training jets. However, except for a small patriotically spirited group which had been imprisoned because of their refusal to bomb the peasants in the Sierra Maestra, most air force personnel had fought on Batista's side. Therefore, we had more planes than pilots, and training a pilot takes time.

The formation of cadres was very important, as I said, and Comrade Fernández was exceptionally helpful in that regard. He was the one who taught everyone here to march, because the members of the Rebel Army didn't know how to stand, how to salute, how to march. Since Fernández had studied in a military academy, he taught us the formalities, the organization of a platoon, a company, a battalion. We had to start organizing the large army we needed from scratch.

Forces were being trained in all the provinces

But when would they come? We did not have the extensive intelligence service we have now; we picked up news, we read. But here's a glimpse of how they controlled the press when they wanted to: In the United States they gave the press instructions not to talk about the organization of the expedition. Something always leaked out, but which plan would it be? Would they attempt to form guerrilla groups in the different regions of the country? They had already formed such groups in the Escambray mountains. In fact, they brought in arms all over the island. We wondered, would it be a generalized guerrilla war? It's always harder to capture a small group than a troop. We wanted them to send them all together, of course. But what would they do? In every cove and on every small beach in the country we put a militia platoon; we left no place unguarded. And of course, forces were being trained in all the provinces.

If they decided to go in one direction, which one would they choose? We thought, for example, that they might try to establish a sort of Taiwan on the Isle of Pines, now called the Isle of Youth. The prisons were there, filled with thousands of counterrevolutionary prisoners and war criminals, so what we did was send tanks, infantry and cannons there and turned the Isle of Pines into a fortress.

Could it be in the Escambray mountains? There was a certain logic to that; they had organized many groups there and at one point had 1,000 armed men in the Escambray who were experts in evading our forces. I will not call them cowards. There can be people who are mistaken, and even very mistaken, who are personally brave but not personally moral; one must never underestimate the enemy. But they were the opposite of us in the Sierra Maestra. In the Sierra Maestra we were always on the offensive, organizing ambushes, organizing strikes, while those people in the Escambray were always running away from the revolutionary troops. They had some help from the campesinos — a minority of them, but support nevertheless — 10, 15 or 20 percent — nobody could say exactly. The war had developed in a different way there than in the Sierra Maestra. There was never the intense political work that had been done in the eastern provinces, and there had even been some abuses committed by the groups in those areas. The Escambray was politically weak so the counterrevolutionaries began there with people disaffected by the revolutionary laws, politically backward people or former members of Batista's army who had gone there.

I repeat, on occasions they had as many as 1,000 men; we would cut them down to 70 or 80, but within a few months, with help from abroad, they would rise up again. But they always had the same defensive strategy, trying to escape, waiting for the U.S. invasion. There was a time when the revolution concentrated 50,000 men in the Escambray — which gives you an idea of their strength. The Escambray was completely surrounded, divided into four parts and we started to clean up, with squadrons going house to house. At some point, the Escambray could have been their preferred spot for launching an invasion, being a mountainous area where motorized forces would have to go up the coast, with its own airport and a certain base of internal support. But the Escambray became another indomitable fortress of the revolution.

This left the Bay of Pigs. There had been nothing there, and in the first year of the revolution we started building roads, in order to improve the lives of the charcoal makers and their families. Three key roads were being built: the one going from Australia [sugar mill] to Playa Larga, Yaguaramas-San Blas, and the other, Covadonga-San Blas. That one was V-shaped and we were pretty well advanced in the construction of two tourism centers. We were also building schools and an airfield. The airfield was necessary for the enemy, for supplying arms and for bringing in the provisional government, which was the real plan to legitimize their crime.

So those days were days of great activity as we confronted the sabotage, the armed groups, the bandits in the countryside. We were waiting for the main attack, wondering how, where and if they would divide those forces they were training abroad or concentrate them; that was key. We had to be prepared for the two variants. If small groups arrived, we had to fight against all the groups that landed. If they concentrated them, we had to have sufficient forces to destroy them. We were expecting an invasion when the early morning bombing occurred on April 15. That was a whopping blunder on the part of the enemy, because by attacking us and inventing that whole thing about the insurgent airplanes, by employing considerable air power, they immediately gave us the idea that the invasion was possible within 24 or 48 hours. Although we had part of the country mobilized, we immediately mobilized the whole country and all the arms.

On April 16, exactly 35 years ago, and I believe more or less at this same time of day, after we buried our comrades, we organized a large rally with tens of thousands of armed militia members on the corner of 12th and 23rd Streets in Havana; they filled up 23rd Street for many blocks. As you can imagine, there was a state of tremendous indignation; the people were inflamed. The revolution had advanced quite a bit; we knew that this was the price they wanted to make us pay for having our revolution, and although many of our measures were simple acts of social justice, they could also rightly be called socialist measures.

Attacks accelerated revolutionary changes

This whole process of attacks against Cuba accelerated revolutionary changes. Some day socialism had to come, but many things needed to be done first. It was not considered to be the moment to talk about socialism. There was an energetic battle against communism, since this was the United States' principal ideological weapon in the Cold War that was in full swing, but socialism was not discussed. On that day, given the realities and the acceleration of that process, the extent of the social justice measures that we had adopted, we considered it within our right to proclaim the socialist nature of the revolution. This was acclaimed throughout the length and breadth of the country by tens of thousands of armed Cubans. If in the Sierra Maestra we were fighting to destroy the [Batista] dictatorship, we were also fighting for social justice and for our country's liberation. From April 17, our people, with arms in their hands and at the cost of their blood, fought for socialism.

In reality, it was the moment to give that energetic, bold, defiant response, because the Bay of Pigs occurred when we were surrounded by the U.S. squadron. It was as if to say to them: if you want to land, do it, we're not afraid of you.

Rapid grasp of the enemy's strategy

Within this whole framework what were the decisive elements? First, the air attack that took place 48 hours before gave us time; it can't be explained why they did this. They wanted to launch a second attack, but they had already failed in the initial attempt. They couldn't destroy any more aircraft because there were anti-aircraft guns protecting the three airports. For that reason they couldn't destroy all the airplanes as the airports were even more reinforced.

As I said, they were considering a second air attack on the morning of April 17; they were not able to carry it out because at dawn on that day all our planes had taken off for the Bay of Pigs to attack the enemy squadron, the fleet that brought the invaders. That was a decisive factor.

Another important factor was the rapid grasp of the enemy's strategy. They began to drop the paratroopers very early in different places. We knew very early on that they had dropped paratroopers, and when they launched their paratroopers, we immediately realized the main direction of their attack. They dropped them over Covadonga, San Blas, Yaguaramas, Pálpite and some close to this side, making it clear that they wanted to take and secure the three access routes by covering both directions of the Ciénaga de Zapata highway.

That Ciénaga swampland cannot be flanked or skirted and anyone attempting to cross it would sink. They had tanks and antitank weapons. It would have been very difficult to recover that position, advancing via the highway. If we'd had to recover it on foot through the Ciénaga, it would have been extremely costly. For that reason, when information reached us in the early morning hours that they were landing, the mobilization in that direction began immediately. The most experienced unit we had at that time was from here in Matanzas, and Fernández was asked to lead it immediately to the zone of operations, to Playa Larga, which was the nearest point. But at that same time, all the tanks and cannons in Havana were being mobilized, all the anti-aircraft weapons, all the battalions, everybody was mobilized. And the ships as well, every unit had to be ready to advance. There were only five transports for the tanks, the rest had to be pulled by their axles, and it was a good distance.

The problem was that the enemy air force was numerous and active. We didn't know how many aircraft they had. We had no means of knowing if they were 20, 30, 40 or 100, nor who was piloting them, because when they ran out of Cuban pilots they started using U.S. pilots. For that reason, all our armaments, the tanks, artillery and infantry were accompanied by anti-aircraft guns. There were a lot of them and they had instructions to advance to Jovellanos. Not knowing the number of possible planes in the air, we couldn't risk sending that troop by day beyond Jovellanos, toward the Bay of Pigs. We asked them to camouflage themselves as best they could and to wait.

Our planes were attacking the squadron, so our soldiers had to endure the air attacks because we didn't have any more planes, and the important thing was to leave the enemy without a squadron. That's why we had casualties, and also because of their trick of using Cuban insignia on their planes.

Not a minute's respite

At dusk the torrent of tanks, artillery and the rest began to advance in that direction, while the people of Villa Clara were also mobilizing. What is now the Central Army, which was founded on April 4, was mobilizing with all its forces to attack in the direction of Covadonga and Yaguaramas. In fact, they fought without rest, because I believe that the third most important element was not to give them a minute's respite. Since the idea was to bring in the provisional government, and then call on the OAS [Organization of American States] to intervene immediately — with only a few token soldiers from each Latin American country and the rest U.S. soldiers — we couldn't give them time to establish a beachhead to land their provisional government.

They were lucky — and I'm not going to explain why now — because we were without communications. We had to communicate by telephone from one town to another as nothing could be said over the radio. In fact, only the tanks and some of the trucks had radios.

They might have lasted at the most 42 hours, except for a maneuver that we had to make. They tricked us, and they tricked us twice — the U.S. troops, not the mercenaries. At the time of the funeral I was speaking and close to finishing when a message arrived that a squadron of ships and some landing craft were approaching from the west of Havana. I said: "What? That's very unusual, it sounds as if they want to start with Havana." The Playa Larga landing had not yet occurred. I recall that I finished that speech rapidly, we played the National Anthem and I don't know if I said *"Patria o muerte."* Anyway, I finished rapidly because of the news we had received and I said: "So, it is beginning today, to the west of Havana." This maneuver was organized by the United States.

On the night of April 17 to 18, when we were in Pálpite, in that area, I received the news of a landing to the west of Havana. I said: "Right, is that confirmed?" They told me, "Yes, it's confirmed, contact with the enemy has already been made." And, filled with resignation we prepared to surround Playa Larga from the west and continue advancing from the east toward the Bay of Pigs before dawn. Those from the Bay of Pigs would have encountered our tanks, they wouldn't have been able to join up. But our tanks took a long time to get here because they were being pulled by their axles. We had to wait there for at least half an hour to an hour, and if the principal battle was going to be in Havana, that maneuver would lose importance. I said, "This is all very strange." But when I reached Havana, I found out there had been no landing.

This was a big disappointment, I assure you, because we had the bulk of our armaments in Havana, including the frigates with all the cannons and the ships. But 10 percent of our forces were mobilized here [in Matanzas], if we do not include the air force. "Well," I said, "who is going to land there in Havana? They are going to take an exceptional thrashing, because Havana's quite close, a four-hour journey speeding along the highway from Havana to here."

So they pulled two maneuvers on us. The first one didn't have much effect because it was soon confirmed that nothing was happening; but the second one meant that what lasted 88 hours should have lasted maybe less than 48, 46 or 44 hours. Every time one remembers this history it's painful, because although they had a good thrashing, we would have liked it to have been more rapid and a more thorough one. We had more casualties than they did, which was logical given that our people were attacking, unprotected on straight roads that could not be flanked and via swampland. Furthermore, they were treacherously hit by aircraft with Cuban insignia.

It's already been explained many times, what everybody did: the Rebel Army and the Ministry of the Interior. Our armed forces were composed of everyone who had a weapon, but we called it a militia. Although armies were already being organized in all the provinces or principal regions, we did not have a level higher than that of battalion; at the Bay of Pigs the highest level was that of the battalion.

Great prowess

I sincerely believe that the Bay of Pigs battle was a great example of our people's prowess. Not only in terms of what they did, but because of what they were prepared to do to ensure that the United States suffered a defeat in Cuba, even if the price for us would have been very high, even if we would have been the first Vietnam. I am talking about hundreds of thousands of arms. We had sufficient to take 10 of the invaders' arms for every one of ours, as happened in the Cuban liberation struggle when of every 10 arms that we had, approximately nine had been taken from our adversary. Cuba would have resisted, but thanks to its heroism that war was prevented.

That was not the only danger: there was the war against subversion, the war against terrorists, the war against bandits. There were times when we had bandit groups in all the provinces of the country, and there were mercenaries and pirate attacks. From time to time, when we heard of plans and received information of danger, we mobilized all the people. The Missile Crisis was the most dramatic demonstration of the great valor of the entire nation under unprecedented circumstances.

We have had to devote many resources and have made many sacrifices in order to defend this country over these years of the revolution, as we have been constantly and steadily more rigorously blockaded by the United States, and then had to face the disappearance of the Soviet Union and the socialist camp. It seems we've gone through a lot, and now nobody knows who to blame for it: Christopher Columbus, who discovered us? The English? Well, they left us here and frankly we are content.

This was the place that fell to us, and history has made this people what we are. It has been a very difficult history: first, the European conquest, the disappearance of practically the entire indigenous population, and afterwards, slavery — hundreds of thousands of slaves. This was one of the provinces where there was a slave society. And then there were the U.S. annexationist attempts throughout the centuries.

Our people's struggles in several wars, including the Ten Years' War, constitute the raw material from which this people is forged. When the countries of Latin America almost simultaneously liberated themselves, Spain reached the point of having more soldiers in Cuba than in all of Latin America — up to 300,000 armed men fighting against a small country. All those historical factors, in my opinion, have made it possible for Cuba to be what it is today. What they wanted to take from us by force on that April 16 with that mercenary invasion, was what they had not been able to take from us with blockades of petroleum, foodstuffs, machinery, with subversive plans. Through that invasion, they wanted to take everything that is now a cause for pride for our country.

Our battle today

I was reading some data: infant mortality is 7.5 [per 1,000 live births] in the first quarter of this year. That's incredible, really. I don't expect we'll be able to maintain it; that would be over-optimistic; but never have we had an infant mortality rate of 7.5 in a period like this. As a health indicator, how many peoples of the world, rich peoples and peoples with resources, have such a figure? In Washington there are over 30 child deaths per 1,000 live births. Clearly, those who die are, in the main, the children of the black population; but also whites, as there are many poor whites, although the former have worse conditions.

We have two million plus students within the educational system, and almost 9,000 primary schools; more than 150,000 children in day-care centers or in preschools; over half a million students at intermediate level, all the special schools, all the art schools and sports schools. What would have remained of our public health system, of our education, of our culture? What would have been left of this country if they had been able to overcome us then?

Our battle today is even more meritorious, if you like, because we are fighting on our own. Previously we were alone, but we believed we were accompanied. Some lessons, like the Missile Crisis and others, taught us otherwise. The accelerated withdrawal of that small brigade which was here. . . Well, that was no secret at the time. For a long time we have known that it was the Cubans, and only the Cubans who were going to defend the country. And only Cubans could defend the country, using the correct tactics, not playing the little war games of Clausewitz, but with a war of all the people.

In that way we made the revolution and defended it, and in that way we will continue defending it. There is no comparison. It's true that those neighbors of ours are becoming more and more crazy and are increasingly more ungovernable. They are more and more politically confused as well as more and more clumsy. That can lead them to commit errors, major errors, and this has to be taken into account.

Are we scared? It's impossible to conceive of fear after all that we have lived through! They will get their world, the world they seek, a world that will be steadily more and more ungovernable, because I am convinced that some governments — many municipal governments in our country — know more about politics than the U.S. administration in Washington. The municipal government governs better than the government of the United States.

They are in chaos, with the country divided between reactionary currents and other more liberal currents, between more sane and less sane people. There are growing ethnic phobias and fascist sentiments and tendencies, and with an enormous strength. They can't even govern themselves, or don't want to govern themselves, on account of the disorder caused by hundreds of billions of dollars' worth of drugs. The disaster of a criminal movement that is growing by the year; that hatred of the poor; that desire to do away with pensions and other social conquests, gained in one form or another by the U.S. people over the decades since the Roosevelt era; that habit of wanting to govern the world, telling everyone what to do; of insulting presidents that they refer to as friends, such as those proconsul statements by U.S. ambassadors, that conduct demonstrated here over the February 24 incident.[4] That was an incident that could have been avoided, an incident that was foreseen by us, an incident that we warned them of on many occasions. And we know a little bit more about that episode, but it's always necessary to keep some truths in reserve. Moreover, one always has to be gentlemanly, even when one has to fight against wretched people.

You saw their behavior, the number of times they violated our airspace, the increasingly more daring flights over our capital, something that no country in the world would permit, and then inventing the lie that those light aircraft were in international waters. These aircraft have been designed for war; they were bought from the U.S. government, which used them in Vietnam. They have attacked us using light aircraft on many occasions, and have even used them in biological warfare against us.

They have used all available means against our country, including the insolence with which they attempted to have us condemned in the Security Council. The fact is that we have a moral standing, a high moral standing, and we speak with truthfulness, and always speak the truth. With the truth and our moral standing we will be invincible, we will win the battles on all the fronts on which we have to fight. We will wait, we are patient, we have learned how to be patient, we have the necessary patience as far as decorum allows. We are not warmongers.

We are happy to celebrate this 35th anniversary of the Bay of Pigs invasion. We are happy about all the lives that were saved. We are happy that our children have grown up healthy, educated and cultured. We are happy about our marvelous young people. Yes, may they live a long time!

We already know that in order to live with dignity in this world, one has to struggle, and you see every day on television what happens in the rest of the world. The other day we saw how some Mexican immigrants were savagely beaten; it was repulsive and something that makes us indignant. One of the immigrants was a woman, and they didn't just hit them once or twice, but five, six, ten times. And all that in front of the television cameras. What must they do off camera? Police cars, police horses, dogs everywhere,

---

[4] On February 24, 1996, two of three planes piloted by the Miami-based "Brothers to the Rescue" were shot down while penetrating Cuban airspace.

strikes every day, people being beaten every day in both developed and poor countries, although it is worse in the poor countries. Theft and more theft, drugs and more drugs, loss of sovereignty and more loss of sovereignty.

It's a shame what goes on in the world, but it can't go on forever. More and more people are gaining consciousness, rising up, those who are sick and tired of seeing a world in which hegemony has been imposed by a power capable of telling lies to the whole world, like those told during the Bay of Pigs invasion — lies that show the lack of scruples and morality that exists within the heart of that empire.

But no matter what difficulties Cubans have, they could never be worse than those of others, when we compare our country's indices with the rest of the Latin American and Third World countries, which are so downtrodden and constantly repressed. Martí said that freedom costs dearly, and that one had to resign oneself to living without it or decide to pay the price.

Our independence requires struggle and sacrifice. Our dignity, our honor, our right to progress, our tomorrow, our future — everything they want to take away from us costs dearly. But all of us, men and women, boys and girls, all of us who have had the privilege of feeling pride, dignity and honor, of feeling what our country is, of feeling all those beautiful things which are worth fighting for, are determined to pay the price, because we will never resign ourselves to living without them.

We face more dangerous mercenaries

Now we must face not the mercenaries who invaded at the Bay of Pigs, but another type of mercenary — mercenaries who want to tighten the blockade, who want to make our people more impoverished by erecting roadblocks on our path to recovering little by little from that great disaster, that tragedy which was the disappearance of the socialist bloc, and turn our people into solitary soldiers. In this case I'm excluding the hundreds of millions of people who sympathize with Cuba and who have turned us into solitary soldiers of humanity's most just cause, clean soldiers, pure soldiers.

We will struggle and stand firm, despite those adversaries to whom I referred and who have threatened us for so many years.

They even dare to threaten us with arms in the Helms-Burton Act. We don't want to fight, we don't want war. We don't have to play at being brave; I don't think even they doubt the courage of our people.

We want peace, and I'm going to repeat the idea: We will work for peace to the extent that our country's honor and dignity and sense of responsibility allow it, because we are not looking for a victory as at the Bay of Pigs, or even 100 victories as at the Bay of Pigs. What we want is peace, our people's health, our people's well-being, our people's lives, which we will risk unhesitatingly only when the price is sovereignty, independence, honor and freedom. I am completely sure that all of you agree with this principle.

Today we have paid tribute to our martyrs. In that way, we have paid tribute, as a comrade said, to all those who died in combat before and after the triumph of the revolution. In that way, we pay tribute to the first Liberation Army fighters who died in our wars of independence. In that way, we pay tribute to those who have died and those who may have to die. In that way, we pay tribute to our heroic people.

For an instant, I try to imagine myself at that moment in which the battalion of those in charge of the militia of that historic school marched to combat at the Bay of Pigs, and didn't stop until it had taken that final, key, decisive point in the battle. Younger and older people like those here today, men and women like yourselves, who went to fight, went to battle, went to die, leaving behind their homes and the people they loved most in the world. A large number died in a short period of time, a large number were wounded in a short period of time.

If there is something we can long for and wish for on an anniversary such as this, it is that you and your compatriots will always be worthy of those fighters, those men and women, that people which has written one of the most brilliant pages in history. Future generations will not think about the size of our neighbor, but the size of this small country, which has stood firm for 35 years and is willing to stand firm for another 35 years, or 35 times 35 years.

Let us state with pride today, the day on which we commemorate the anniversary in which the socialist nature of our revolution was proclaimed for the first time; let us reaffirm as in those days certain of victory:

Socialism or death!

Patria o muerte! [Homeland or death!]

Venceremos! [We will win!]

Trade union congress

Speech of April 30, 1996

In this speech, President Fidel Castro addresses the closing session of the 17th Congress of the Central Organization of Cuban Workers (CTC).

It is not so easy to make a closing speech at a congress such as this, at a time like this, in the complex situation in which we are living; but for any person it is a very great honor to be granted such a privilege, because I believe it is one of the best congresses that I've seen. In the first place, it is a political congress, a revolutionary congress, an ideological congress. It was expressed accurately and profoundly when this congress was described not as a congress of workers demanding a share of the power, or struggling to obtain power, but rather a congress of workers in power.

We have learned many things during these years of intense revolutionary struggle, but here we have learned new things, because we — or at least I — have never had such a clear impression of the nature of a people in power as we have seen in this congress. It is not only that the workers are in power, but that the workers have been in power for 37 years, and are the living expression of the work undertaken during those years. We have seen a number of workers' congresses, but the statistics here are so eloquent: so many university graduates among the delegates, so many intermediate level graduates, and not a single illiterate person, not a single person who does not know what he or she is doing, or why he or she is doing it. That is why this congress has been so moving and so stimulating.

The experience accumulated over years has also been brought to bear here. That was demonstrated from the first day, because — as was so well expressed — it has not been a four-day congress, it has been a year-long congress. In one year the Cuban trade unions worked in a truly admirable way to guarantee the quality of this event. You certainly haven't been on vacation, because throughout this special period you have had to participate in supremely important processes, in very hard tasks as part of this major battle for the survival of the revolution and of the nation, first in the workers' parliaments and then in the assemblies for efficiency.

Defending many sacred things

We cannot forget that we were confronted by practically insoluble problems. What could we do when the country was left on its own, losing everything overnight: markets, raw materials, fertilizers, fuel, credits? We were also blockaded, and on top of that, morally battered. It was a very hard blow for all of us to see those who had been our allies in the struggle collapsing, while the United States was emerging stronger, wealthier and more influential than ever.

In that situation we had the sacred duty of defending many sacred things: we had to defend the nation, the country's history, the revolution, the country's independence, dignity and even its life, because can any of you conceive of life without the revolution? Could the millions and millions of patriots who have fought for so long conceive of life without the revolution? So, the very life of a people was at stake in a unipolar world, on a little island without big rivers, without its own fuel, without large natural resources, and living next door to a power that did not easily resign itself to this country's existence, to this country's valor, to this country's challenge and this country's victories. That power has never given up the idea of destroying the revolution and its achievements.

New information is appearing all the time, with the publication of some files and documents relating to the many operations they have carried out against us. This people has had to take on the taming of not just one, two or three tigers, but of a thousand tigers. Somebody once said that it was a paper tiger and, in the strategic sense, it is. One day it will cease to be master of the world. Meanwhile, this little country has had to fight every day since January 1,

1959, throughout the Cold War, facing this monstrous force, which is equivalent to having to tame I don't know how many beasts on countless occasions.

I think that deep down, despite their haughtiness, arrogance and the tendency to belittle others, they are not scornful of this country or this people. However, without any doubt we will have to continue playing our role as lion tamers for a long time; and I believe that the lion tamers to come, male and female, will be better lion tamers than us. That's our hope, and that hope is strengthened when we have the opportunity of participating in an event such as this.

During these long years, who knows how many measures they have taken against us. We are certain that they have even resorted to bacteriological warfare against our country, which has affected plants, animals and human beings.

How it must pain them that at this congress we can speak of an infant mortality rate of under 10, and even under nine, after five years of the special period! How painful must be the news that life expectancy has increased and that in spite of the shortage of resources and medicines, our doctors are constantly making ever greater advances!

How can this Cuban miracle be compared with what we know is occurring in other parts of the world and particularly in Latin America? They have wanted to destroy our country, they have even wanted to charge us with human rights violations, when the lives of approximately one million children and young people have been saved by the work of the revolution. That reduction in infant mortality in the first year of life from 60 to less than 10 signifies hundreds of thousands of babies' lives saved, to which can be added the hundreds of thousands over one year of age who have been saved, and all the lives saved by the revolution, as evidenced by the raising of life expectancy by 20 years for our compatriots.

The United States supported all the bloody regimes responsible for the disappearance of tens of thousands of people — some people affirm that it was hundreds of thousands, because there are countries where over 100,000 people disappeared after U.S. intervention, as was the case in Guatemala — with their arms, advisers and torture methods. Everything they learned in the war in Vietnam was then taught to the repressive forces in Latin America in order to prevent another Cuban revolution. It didn't matter to them if 100 infants out of every thousand or more died each year.

If we have the right to talk of having saved the lives of hundreds of thousands of children, we can also say that thanks to U.S. policies, during the lifetime of the Cuban revolution tens of millions of children have died in Latin America, and are still dying. They are living in steadily worsening conditions, dying from old and new diseases. Can there be any moral comparison between the socialism we have been building with so much sacrifice and heroism, and the imperialism and capitalism that they represent? All this must hurt them a lot, as well as comparisons with other things that are happening in this unipolar world.

Recently you all read that a number of people in England fell sick with an illness that attacks the brain. This is a fairly well-known disease which also affects other species, such as sheep and cattle. When there were 10 or 12 cases in young people, a terrible panic broke out in Europe and almost in the whole world, and there was talk of slaughtering millions of head of cattle in places like England.

During that same period, after the first news of that disease in England, between 8,000 and 10,000 people died of meningitis in West Africa, without immunization or medical care. What would happen in Europe if 8,000 or 10,000 people died of a similar illness within a few weeks? However, what occurred in Africa went practically unmentioned. How could the world achieve such a level of selfishness, such a lack of solidarity, that such things can happen? Thus, diseases such as AIDS and others are on the increase; cholera, tuberculosis, this latter also associated with AIDS, and terrible problems of that type are appearing. That's of no importance to them.

How they must suffer knowing that, in spite of their blockade of so many years, the collapse of the socialist bloc and the special period, we have been able to guarantee, in one form or another, one liter of milk per day to all children under seven years of age, and a considerable quantity of yogurt to children between the ages of seven and 13, at prices totally accessible to the population.

This country is growing stronger
There is hatred for Cuba and at the same time respect, as I was saying. Contempt there cannot be, but there is a hatred for this country

that they believed would fall a few days after the collapse of the socialist bloc and the Soviet Union. But they are seeing the years pass by without it collapsing; on the contrary, and without exaggeration, it is stronger and beginning to advance. It must really be unbearable.

They invent legislation and other measures such as the Torricelli Act, to destroy us from within, or to destroy us through hunger, through total economic strangulation. There are even lunatics who are thinking along the lines of destroying us by force, without the least sense of responsibility for the implacable hornet's nest they would stir up in Cuba and, I am sure, on the whole continent if the craziness of a military action against our country was one day implemented. They come up with new legislation, a more rigorous blockade, new measures, a lot of pressure exerted on the world, anything rather than renouncing their obsessive idea of eliminating the revolution.

The sentiment of our workers and of our people has been expressed here energetically, patriotically, militantly, with a willingness to work hard and a very profound comprehension of the historical period we are living through, and of the extremely difficult battle that has to be waged.

All of that was expressed in the congress — and in the ideas clearly expressed by Pedro Ross[1] with your unanimous support, and discussed in the theses and supported in the assemblies — to the effect that what we are doing is socialism, and what we want is socialism, and what we are defending is socialism, so that nobody should be left in any doubt. It is socialist Cuba, that power of the people and those achievements of the revolution that we are defending. I agree with what a woman comrade said this afternoon, that the first achievement was precisely the revolution itself: the power of the people. This sentiment was expressed today as never before.

We have recovered so much morally, politically, in terms of awareness, from that crushing blow we received five or six years ago. It has been demonstrated — making another Olympic allusion — that our country as a boxer has a tough, tough jaw; it's impossible to knock it out. It resisted, it withstood the ideological blow and was able to resist heroically the tremendous material blow it received.

---

[1] Pedro Ross is the General Secretary of the CTC (Central Organization of Cuban Workers) and a member of the Political Bureau of the Communist Party of Cuba.

This can be clearly perceived in the tone, the spirit and the dignity of the discussions here, which leads to the primary conclusion that the revolution at this moment is stronger than ever.

A new spirit has emerged

This congress has also been a highly important economic and social congress. During this year-long process, every possible subject has been discussed, including problems with major implications. The progress of the renewed effort in the sugar harvest, the planting, the weeding, the harvesting have all been discussed across the length and breadth of the island. Many ideas have been developed, a great deal of knowledge has been acquired and a new spirit has emerged. The spirit with which our people have worked over the last six to seven months or more — since June–July — planting, weeding, constantly mobilizing for that task, is a spirit that had not been seen for a long time, if indeed ever before. That same spirit has been shown in the disposition of the workers during the harvest, a harvest that has many difficulties accumulated from previous years, in cane fields that hadn't been harvested in four or five years. Where the best harvesters couldn't cut, there have been men and women cutting cane in this difficult harvest.

This battle is not won in a day! We had to deal with I don't know how many machines without parts; harvesters which had gone for many years without any repairs; no steel for the repairs; no steel for the sugar mills; no resources to buy engines and replace engines. The harvest was carried out with the resources we found as we went along, because we have resisted, given that the revolution didn't collapse a few days after the disappearance of the socialist bloc.

Business people and the world came to gain confidence in Cuba and in Cuba's capacity to fight and to resist. Resources began to appear which we couldn't have even thought about in the early years: financing for tobacco cultivation, for cane, for rice and then for new products, significant credits of a notable volume, although in real terms we have to pay dearly for them, paying them back at higher interest rates. No other country has to pay the interest rates that we are paying for those credits. That's the blockade, those are the pressures, that's the price that we have to pay for every one of these steps we have taken to obtain resources. We're doing it, and in this way we have started to increase production with minimal resources.

You see what can be done today with a ton of fuel, with a ton of steel; we do three times as much as before with the machines we have available. We made those gains and won those possibilities with our fortitude, with our resistance, and that exasperates them.

In other countries they have spent billions to eradicate socialism — they have lent it, donated it and given it away and, in exchange, production has fallen even lower and lower. There was a time when our production lacked everything: fuel, raw materials for the textile industry and the machine industry, for numerous lines of manufacture, for the production of milk, meat, eggs and imported animal feed. Factories were completely paralyzed for lack of electricity and there were neither materials to repair them nor sufficient fuel for minimum needs. So many factories had to close down.

And transportation: we saw how the almost 30,000 daily journeys within the City of Havana were reduced to 6,000 or 7,000. The country has had to acquire or manufacture two million bicycles to confront the transportation problems of workers, students and people who needed mobility. Two million bicycles! We set about improvising bicycle factories to produce some of them, searching for all kinds of solutions.

The loss of raw materials for footwear, clothing, everything — such a material blow really could not be conceived. You have seen how factories that were paralyzed have been made operational again; how raw materials have been appearing; how the machine industry is recovering; how the nickel industry is recovering; how sugar production is recovering; and how food production is recovering. Miracles are being worked in transportation; because what we were told yesterday about the contributions from this sector, the expenditure required had been saved, and what they are contributing now is virtually incredible. They are now being asked for 60 million in convertible currency for medicines. How the scientists, researchers and others have worked to find all sorts of solutions, from medicines to machinery and parts, etc.

All those things are visible. However, one thing has a stronger claim on my attention: the reaction of the people, how we are beginning to see a heartening and healthy state that has been developing since the most critical moments, since the time we were in intensive care. We can observe what the people have learned and how the idea of economic efficiency, one of the most important and most decisive results of this congress, has taken hold. Controls, savings, efficiency, loss reduction, increased earnings, profitability, the fight for enterprise profitability, the tremendous battle to save a factory, to keep it from closing because of its economic and social importance, all this can now be observed. The spirit of studying every aspect, that process which has been referred to as the reordering of the work force and that famous phrase you use: the redirecting of enterprises.

We can talk about all of that without embarrassment or shame, because we have done everything I've been talking about on our own. When I say on our own, I'm not including our sympathizers, the labor, political and all the other kinds of organizations that have expressed so much solidarity and affection for Cuba; I mean alone as a country faced with this situation, which is unprecedented anywhere and at any time in history.

We have confronted the problems. It is the reverse of what happens everywhere else and of what is advised everywhere else by the World Bank, the International Monetary Fund and the United States. All those neoliberal theories that you're familiar with, all those practices, throwing tens of millions of workers onto the streets, closing schools, closing hospitals, eliminating essential public services, without consulting anybody.

Consulting with the people
We could say that in this whole process of the special period, not a single step was taken without consulting the people, especially the workers. It has been a long process and we have had to adapt ourselves to unpleasant realities which make us suffer like someone in an intensive care unit, or in a state of severe crisis.

We also had to resign ourselves to many things that we didn't want to accept, educated as we were in a great spirit of equality, of equal opportunities for all, which we were able to enjoy for a number of years, at that stage of world development.

Ramón [Castro] and others spoke of a mental blockade, but in our minds we had a number of things, a number of good things. This people's spirit of solidarity has no parallel: its generosity, its willingness to help and give, its love of justice; that communist spirit of our people. We had a communist spirit without an economy that could permit communism, and for that reason we always explained that socialism was one thing and communism was another.

Now we are applying the ideas of socialism much more consistently. Before there was also idealism, wasn't there? And there were possibilities. We had so many resources that sometimes we squandered them. Nevertheless, the people created a spirit of equality, justice, a consciousness of their rights as citizens, as human beings. The revolution never failed in its zeal to support the people, and to do what it could for the people and for each of its citizens, even more than we were able to do.

The revolution achieved all these things that no other Third World country has attained and that, in fact, many peoples have not attained. In social achievements, almost no other people in the world have attained them. At this moment I can't forget Vietnam, I can't forget China, countries which made enormous efforts as we did, under difficult conditions. But what capitalist country achieved the level of social security, of social justice, of respect for the people?

Some very rich people — and they became rich at the expense of the underdevelopment of the rest of the world — had so much money and were so afraid of communism and socialism that they tried to implement a better distribution of the resources they had. However, now the Cold War is over, now the socialist bloc has collapsed, and now measures are taken without concern for any class. The capitalists and imperialists have gone so far with their neoliberal measures that today even the International Monetary Fund speaks of social development, because it sees that the world is turning into a volcano as the situation is so unbearable.

Neoliberalism and the globalization of the economy

It is clear that the exploiters are starting to get afraid again. They are afraid of social upheaval, afraid of social explosions, afraid of chaos, fears they had lost when they believed they could commit injustices in this world with greater freedom than ever. Now they are afraid again, so the International Monetary Fund, the World Bank and other institutions are speaking about the need to dedicate resources to social development.

Neoliberalism, the globalization of the economy, hegemonic policies, selfishness and the monopoly of all the resources are incompatible with social development. To tell the truth, no one knows what's happening with the money that these institutions, as a whole, intend to devote to social development. Furthermore, a huge wave of corruption has been unleashed, and not just in Latin American countries or African countries, but also in Europe and the developed world. There are also waves of violence, drug consumption and social measures to achieve balanced budgets. They are reducing workers' pensions, public health spending for retired people. We see this problem quite frequently in Europe where they are merciless in their desire to balance their budgets, at the expense of social rights.

In the United States, there is a barbarous wave of measures to cut social benefits to the detriment of retired workers, the elderly, the sick, everyone. They are doing away with anything that hints of progressive politics in all these countries, in order to impose savage, merciless capitalism, with a fanatical faith that the laws of the market will solve everything. For that reason, they are not in the state of euphoria and exhilaration that they were five years ago. Now they are full of worry because they don't really know what's going to happen.

What a difference this is from what has happened in Cuba during the special period. We had to take steps, many difficult measures. As someone who spoke on behalf of the foreign delegates said yesterday, in other countries a few people get together to decide on measures that are then applied mercilessly, with policemen on horseback, with tear gas, with police cars. We see that on television every day in the news from abroad. That's how they impose their measures. How different from the manner in which the revolution undertook to solve the terrible economic situation! First of all, no one was thrown into the street; workers in the factories that were shut down continued to get paid, maybe not 100 percent, but a large part of their previous income, at least a sufficient amount for the few things that could be bought. No one was abandoned.

Of course, the financial situation created was very difficult, because if no one is thrown into the street, people must be paid, and that created a situation in which the currency in circulation inevitably suffered a very large increase. The only other way is what the capitalist countries do: workers thrown out on the street and millions of people left unprotected. A revolution does not do that and cannot do that. To do that would not only be counterrevolutionary, but also stupid, to say the least. A revolution, and certainly not this one, could not adopt measures of that kind, and none of us were willing to adopt measures of that kind. At the time there were all kinds of advisers, but we stood our ground; we did things as we thought they should be done. Everything was discussed in the National Assembly, in the streets, again in the National Assembly, again in the streets — all the measures and economic opportunities, the joint ventures, the possibilities for foreign investment and everything we have been doing in order to face the situation in a way we considered correct.

Money in circulation had to be reduced

The financial situation had reached a critical point, which couldn't continue: 12 billion pesos in the street. At a time when we needed more than ever to work, many people were leaving their jobs, because one person's wages were enough to satisfy a family's needs. At the very moment when workers were needed, people were leaving their workplaces left, right and center.

On top of all this there was the transportation crisis. It was terrible. We began to win the battle using revolutionary and democratic methods, and the amount of money in circulation began to be reduced.

But remember all the measures we discussed and how many millions of people expressed their views; how, finally, measures were taken which had been discussed and which had gained widespread consensus. Some of them were extremely hard, not those related to food, but to cigarettes and alcoholic beverages. These are things that hurt and that have an influence.

Of course, the money collected in our sports facilities does not amount to much — the gate charge for a baseball game between Industriales and Pinareños does not cost 20 pesos — but it was educational. These charges hurt us a lot, even though they are next to nothing: 20 cents or so for a school lunch. They didn't solve the problem; many of the measures taken brought in only small amounts. Others did bring in a lot, such as the price increases on cigarettes and alcoholic beverages. There were 12 billion pesos on the street.

Other measures were adopted, such as the farmers' markets, to give impetus to food production, to open up the possibility of being able to buy some things which were impossible to obtain, given the situation we were in. Clearly, these were not the methods we had used before, when we could distribute pork, chicken, eggs, milk and other foodstuffs at minimum prices, which was a better way. Nor did we have the resources to establish parallel markets to bring in capital for the state. Nevertheless, we had to find a way of making that money circulate better, to collect a little money. Moreover, many people were absolutely convinced that the farmers' markets were a solution, since people had a lot of money in their pockets, but didn't have anything to spend it on. They were saying, "It's better to have somebody supplying something, never mind the price. . ." There are criticisms of the markets because of the prices, but as I understand it, many people who complain about the market also defend it.

For me, it is not an ideal solution, far from it. But it was a measure that had to be taken, with its advantages and disadvantages. The middle person inevitably emerged and remains because this is a personality associated with the free market. Many people say the prices have to be brought down. From the moment you start to regulate the prices there, you'll see what happens. It's like regulating the black market: either you establish that measure and the prices are free, or you don't establish it. The fact is that many people began to pick mangoes, guavas and other fruits and vegetables that were not being harvested, to sell in the farmers' markets.

The situation had reached the point where one dollar was worth practically 150 pesos. Incredible! And it was being changed on the streets. Now there are places where you can freely exchange dollars and pesos. The convertible peso, used in certain forms of incentives, was also established, together with other measures. Several measures were put into effect, after trial runs in some cases; at times, nobody knew what was going to happen.

Of course, one thing was inevitable: people began to spend money. In the first year almost two billion pesos were brought in, I think it was 1.953 billion; in the second year it was about 700 million, already reduced by almost two-thirds because, naturally, money was being spent. A relatively significant portion was recovered by the state which was anti-inflationary. Another far smaller portion was recovered by the state in taxes and other measures imposed on the farmers' markets and on self-employed workers. An even smaller portion by the UBPCs,[2] as they are new organizations; and another by state companies. It was appropriate that they should recover money.

However, one of the sacred things that we had to defend was the ration system still available to the population, to guarantee that minimum amount of garden and root vegetables and other food products where possible. A significant proportion of these foodstuffs are imported. This meant guaranteeing rice and specific quantities of imported beans. Over 80 percent of the production of the UBPCs, of the cooperatives and of the remaining state enterprises all reached the population at local distribution points, and this year we've seen the miracle of non-rationed products, even if these are only cabbage and potatoes.

The organic farms began to produce results everywhere, they took off in almost all parts of the country. Fresh vegetables began to appear at good prices, as a consequence of all those measures. Most of what was sold in the farmers' markets came from the private farmers, and was brought there by middle people who up until now didn't pay taxes, but they will have to do so.

Theft makes things more expensive, not taxes

Those sectors that do not want to pay taxes have created myths and confusion in relation to taxes. They say taxes make things more expensive. What makes things more expensive is theft, not taxes. That cabbage which was being sold at just 15 centavos, or that plantain selling at five centavos — did some tax make them more expensive? It is increased production that is able to reduce the prices.

With the farmers' markets, and similarly with some of the industrial markets, and other forms of high individual earnings, signifi-

---

[2] Basic Units of Cooperative Production were formed when the majority of Cuba's state farms were reorganized into a new cooperative structure in 1993. Unlike the state farms, they own their harvest and now work 42 percent of Cuba's arable land.

cant differences have emerged in the population's income. In the case of the currency in circulation that has been recovered, this in part has been concentrated in an emerging nouveau riche sector.

A taxation system is very logical and is supremely fair. Don't ever let those sectors deceive a worker by putting the blame on taxes when theft is the cause, because they don't want to pay taxes. We'll be in a fine fix if we allow a rich sector to emerge, which could wind up having millions if we're not careful, leaving us with the responsibility of paying for day-care centers, schools, hospitals, polyclinics, family doctors and all the social services provided by the revolution, things which it would never renounce. We'd much rather prevent the emergence of millionaires.

You can be sure that none of us shed a tear because there are no millionaires, although we know many honorable campesinos who have worked with the revolution for many years, who obey the country's laws, who are efficient and who do not speculate or steal, and who have made a lot of money.

The fair prices that the state always paid, especially in the case of those who owned enough land, made that possible. It does not bother us that those families have high incomes. A person can work honorably and also fulfill with pleasure his or her most elementary duties to society. But there are some who charge whatever they please for any product or service.

They exist, and they are getting rich, especially now that their money also has a value, because whoever had 150 pesos before could get one dollar, and now they can get one dollar for 22 or 23 pesos. Our rich are getting richer with the unavoidable measures we have had to take, and we have to understand this; but they are also getting richer because the peso is acquiring value, and that's not a bad thing. What is worrying is that the rich who have easy access to pesos are getting richer, and that's the truth.

However, we must point out that the wages earned by a worker with his own sweat are also taking on value, although he or she receives far less than the rich. We have nothing against rich people; what we want is for them to not steal from the people and that they pay taxes. Some people say: "Why don't they set a price for their products and services?" Who can set a price for them if the individuals go to solve a problem here and there and deal privately with somebody and then they come to an agreement? Who's going to be regulating the repair of a box spring mattress or an old jalopy? However, we can say: You have to pay taxes. Taxation is the way to recoup the abusive excess money that some people are taking in.

Of course, it hurts all of you and it hurts us that the wages we are able to pay many workers in this country are inferior to what some people here earn in one day. There are people here who earn up to 500 pesos in one day — and more — such as the owner of a vehicle who for moving some family, leaves them completely broke, almost in the position of having to leave the furniture in the car in order to pay the charges. You know there are people like that.

Thus, I was telling you that we've introduced measures that are tough, that are not adapted to our mentality, nor to our concepts, but they are inevitable, they had to be established.

So, the buses stopped in Las Tunas, and the horse-drawn carriages appeared. They solved the problem, but the drivers were charging one peso for a 10-minute journey, and taking in 3,000 to 4,000 pesos per month. The People's Power delegates over there wanted to charge higher taxes, in line with what had been established. The taxation system I'm referring to is not easy. It needs to be very well organized, very well controlled, very well studied, and those measures had to be implemented before the complete organizational structure for collecting taxes was set up. But it has been organized, because if all the money accumulated in the hands of a few people in a short time, how could we improve somebody's wages, given the great needs that we have at this time? We haven't had as much success with everything as we have had with the cabbages and plantains, although one day we will.

But one thing is certain already, as production levels have increased in the UBPCs, in the cooperatives, among the campesinos, and even in the victory gardens, the crops grown for a workplace's own consumption, the organic farms, prices in the farmers' markets have seen a parallel drop, as you all know. They have fallen not only because of increased production, but also because there is less money in circulation. So somebody who bought a mango for 20 pesos on the first day won't buy it now for more than one peso.

The people used to say: "What I've got here is just paper, so I'm going to convert it into mangoes, or papayas, or into a pound of pork." Those meat products are the most difficult, for they are not produced in the organic farms; pigs and chickens need feed and other things which are hard to get. Even so, some meat products have fallen in price, for two reasons: increased production and reduced currency in circulation. Nevertheless, it's very important that you understand that the money in circulation has not been reduced sufficiently. I already said that in the first year we brought in almost two billion pesos, the second year it was about half that amount; in short, of the almost 12 billion originally in circulation, about 2.8 billion pesos have been recovered.

Naturally, after a time, the selling prices set by the state, which were bringing in higher sums, began to attract less sales; cigarette sales declined, the obsession passed, there was less money, the price was maintained and health improved. I'm not referring to financial health, but human health, given that we're talking about cigarette smoking in terms of cancer and other diseases. Nowadays, income from cigarette sales is half, or less than half, of former totals, and alcoholic beverages and many other things are also less than half. Charging taxes certainly does not compensate, since taxation is still not being fully implemented. Who knows how many people have not been taxed, because there was no time to organize the collection of taxes from tens of thousands of self-employed workers and people with one type of business or other, and from the middle people.

One of the issues that we have to introduce into our compatriots' consciousness is taxation, something we're not accustomed to in this country, especially after 37 years of the revolution. I'm not talking about across-the-board taxation, that's not what's important. This was fully discussed by the CTC in the context of social security. You have seen how that budget's growing, so that some contribution from the workers was essential. It was even agreed to. We haven't wanted to rush into that, especially in a situation where money is growing more scarce, but we are ready to implement it at any time. That measure has not been applied in haste.

However, there are problems that we must solve. The social security system has to be backed in some way, as it is something that has steadily grown more expensive, and that has been abused in some cases. We heard the painful truth that the number of people retired for total disability has dramatically increased. We have even thought about the idea of reviewing those cases, at least for educational purposes, because the idea that one-third of the retired persons were declared totally incapacitated before reaching retirement age demonstrates disorganization, a lack of control, the immorality of some doctors who are signing certificates, and the lack of an appropriate mechanism so that retirement for reasons of total disability is granted only in genuine cases. This is one of the things that we Cubans do and that costs us very dearly, in millions and millions of pesos.

In this congress, we've talked about everybody who receives assistance, families who receive assistance from social security, and we need revenue for these services. Other solutions have been sought: specific sales, specific products; stores that have been established to bring in capital, which sell in pesos some products normally sold in convertible currency, at higher prices. Money is still coming in, but each time in smaller amounts.

We must reduce the currency in circulation

There is one thing about which we must all be convinced: we cannot return to the situation we had at one point. We cannot renounce the need to reduce the currency in circulation to suitable amounts if we want the peso to continue increasing in value and if we want potential investors to have confidence in us. The demand for investments, in tourism and other sectors, has been advancing rapidly despite the unending pressures and measures imposed by the United States. The increased value of the peso established a confidence in those credits and loans. No other country has achieved what we have in terms of increasing the value of its national currency in the course of a year and a half.

When we explain this to visitors, business people, what the country achieved, they can hardly believe it. When these measures began, the budget deficit was equivalent to 34 percent of the gross domestic product — a colossal sum — and this year it will almost certainly be below 5 percent. Just look at what a major effort we have made in this field, not only in collecting money, but also in saving, pressuring, persuading, in order to reduce the subsidies to factories, agriculture and industry in general. Billions of pesos have been cut, because if we didn't we would be taking in money with one hand and tossing it into circulation with the other. José Luis [Rodríguez, Minister of Finance] says that the budget deficit dropped from five billion to 500 million.

This boosts confidence, stimulates loans, financing, joint ventures and all the activities with which we are defending ourselves. Of course, there are factors which help us. Our neighbors to the north are increasingly making themselves everybody's enemy; they are more and more hegemonic and arrogant, meriting the whole world's ill will and lack of sympathy. The world does not want to be ruled as badly as it is being ruled now. The United States rules the world, but every day more people make up their minds to ignore them, to defy or oppose them. This does not mean that we underestimate their strength and influence, which are very great. But we see the number of disaffected people in the world growing like wildfire, so that people are proposing new ways to invest in Cuba and do business in Cuba, since the measures taken by the United States are more and more absurd.

The Helms-Burton Act has the purpose of halting all that, of preventing a single cent from being lent to Cuba, of making sure that no one dares to invest in Cuba. Yet, here is something paradoxical. I was thinking today, "Wow! These people, Helms and Burton, are defending socialism in Cuba." I mean it. They are defending socialism, because a joint venture by nature has capitalist aspects, and part of the investment of many of the commercial operations is in some way capitalist. But Helms, Burton and company want 100 percent pure socialism in Cuba because they don't want anyone to invest here.

We will wage this great historic battle as well, because we are not abandoning what we're doing, we're just getting started. We'll see what's going to happen with all these new measures, who's going to win this battle and how it will be won, after the passage of that monstrous law which damages the sovereignty of all the other nations in the world. Sovereignty is something which all nations protect very carefully. As I said, although many nations are being dominated, they want a minimum of autonomy. The poorest countries aspire to less, and those with more power aspire to greater autonomy.

Of course, there are serious conflicts among the great economic powers. That is a law which was discovered by Lenin a long time ago, the economic conflicts among these countries, and sometimes what they create is a dogfight for markets and raw materials.

Conflicts among the capitalists

No one should think that life is happy, and although at one point they were super-euphoric, now they are more depressed because of what has happened, despite all the money they spent to dismantle socialism. They see that production is not going up, but instead production is falling, that their illusions are more and more expensive, that capitalism does not solve anything. Not only where there was socialism, but also where there was capitalism, they are now going to ruin. So they are embittered by these things, and also by their inter-capitalist conflicts and rivalries.

Meanwhile, the Cuban revolution goes on, and not a single school has been closed, not a single day-care center, not a single home for the elderly, not a single preschool, not a single institute or educational facility, not a single scientific center. In fact, there are many more scientific centers now. In some places, we have extra capacity in the schools. Of course, we would have continued to build schools to replace the old ones with new ones, but the ones we have are all in operation. Not a single polyclinic or hospital has been shut down, not one! No family doctor has had to leave his post, not one! On the contrary, incredibly, we have more family doctors than before, as the comrade who spoke for the health sector told us today. We have reduced the number of admissions to the medical schools because before we had other considerations, like how many doctors we needed to go abroad, although we are now being asked for doctors.

For example, South Africa has asked for 600 doctors, for which it will pay a reasonable price, of course. The first doctors are already there — I think there are 70 — and soon there will be several hundred. They are also going to give a part of the doctors' income to the Cuban public health system.

We can do with doctors what we do with teachers and professors, giving them advanced study courses, converting that scientific strength into an instrument for the medical personnel's further advancement and retraining. It is much more reasonable to have a person trained as a doctor than to have an ignorant lumpen on the streets. True, there are many fewer admissions. In a certain sense, we have exchanged quantity for quality, since we have more demanding requirements for entering the universities.

We have achieved all this in the context of what is happening in the world, in this country that they left without anything. I ask again what they would say if they heard the delegates talking here about cutting down spiny marabú bushes by hand. Listen, if cane grew as easily as marabú, we could flood the world with sugar. Those bushes grow by themselves!

I had the urge to ask those comrades from Guantánamo and other places when they talked, who planted the marabú? Because it's as if for the past five or six years we had concentrated on growing marabú. And what a brave battle to confront the marabú with a machete and an ax! What a good idea of using it as fuel like firewood for cooking, for all those things! What a valiant job!

What we heard here today was truly admirable. That's why I spoke of the economic and social importance of what you have discussed throughout the year and above all in this congress. I really admired what I heard about the contingent from Santiago de Cuba that's working in Ciego de Avila, what it has done, the fact that it has done so through its own willpower and persistence; what the Mambisa Division in Holguín has done, in a relatively short time and in the midst of heavy rainfall; what the comrades from Guantánamo said about what they were doing; and what the comrades from the UBPCs have said. We heard things we had never heard before, and I know that spirit reigns throughout the country and especially in the provinces. The struggle in the capital is always a little harder, with more problems. But from their visits to the provinces, the comrades from the Political Bureau all bring back very favorable impressions of the spirit prevailing there.

Previously, no one could conceive of any project without bulldozers. In any case, we can't send to the Antillana Steelworks the bulldozers [Alfredo] Jordán [Minister of Agriculture] says he still has left. They would have to get the spare parts. He knows how many spare parts must be obtained in order to get them running. Some of these provinces that make efforts of that kind, if they can hand over a bulldozer or two, they should do so. It's only right, they should have them available.

I want all of you to know that the revolution bulldozed the marabú areas and planted grass, rice, cane and all kinds of things. I remember that brigade which, with hundreds of bulldozers, got all the way to Pinar del Río. The revolution also built dams and many things, but there were many resources, a lot of fuel, a lot of trucks, a lot of spare parts and money. The miracle is that now we're doing what we're doing with the resources we have and with the awareness that we can do much more and we can be more efficient.

We are truly on the right path, and it's an enormous pleasure to see how our working class understands this. With that, we've got the battle won. That same spirit must emerge within the state administrative bodies and People's Power, which are also using new work methods established by the party. That will be achieved to the extent that the party, with greater experience, assumes its obligations, provides support, monitors everything that is being done, and then applies its experience.

We must not lose a minute

Not all lands are alike, not all crops are alike. I think Jordán knows a lot about this, along with Comrade Nelson [Torres, Minister of the Sugar Industry], in terms of taking any positive experience to the provinces. We can't go crazy and say that we're going to do everything in one year, but we must not lose a minute in extending these positive experiences. A positive experience in sugarcane is the recovery of the land. You can't imagine how much is saved and what it signifies.

Yesterday we talked of millions of additional tons of sugar needed. A large part of that is hidden in the weeds that grow alongside the cane, in addition to a few more hectares that must be planted — and we must plant all we can — as well as the way it is done, the seriousness with which it is done, the application of fertilizers and herbicides, the use of drainage wherever possible. Along with all these measures, we can obtain those millions of tons. We have them, they are there, but it depends a lot on us, on our efforts.

This month of May [1996] we are in is tremendous. Some inopportune little rainfalls have appeared here and there, reducing the pace of the cutting and the harvest in almost all the provinces. The rain wasn't announced by the National Observatory, but we can't expect the Observatory to be psychic; they help all they can. But we must till and finish tilling and prepare the land with machines. We must plant, we must weed, we must fertilize, do all those things that were mentioned here and also finish the harvest.

The harvest has these problems I have mentioned. I can give you a positive statistic: as of today there were 4.15 million tons. That means with 350,000 more tons of sugar we will reach the minimum goal we had set ourselves. We say this is minimum, it all depends on the climate and the circumstances. There's enough cane for a little more, but if the rains come they not only block the work but also reduce the sugar content. It's not the same to grind with 12 percent as with 10 percent sugar content.

It is indispensable for us to achieve these proposed goals, because they also play a part in everything else I explained: the confidence in us, the financing, both of which we need so much. That's why this month of May is going to be a month of a lot of work, and very hard work. June and the other months are also important, but this one will be decisive, because we have to cultivate the cane planted in April, which can be cut. Whatever we can plant in the first half of May will be very important.

Now we're anxious to see what the workers from Santiago de Cuba will achieve in Ciego de Avila with their cucumber, cabbage, early potatoes and other things. We're anxious to see how the quality tests on the outer tobacco leaves come out in other provinces. There's a tremendous demand for Cuban cigars, tremendous! The supply does not meet the demand. What we need is more outer leaves; we must grow more because the outer leaves are a valuable commodity, they are not everyday tobacco. We're anxious to see how all the rice-growing programs are going, to raise the large portion of the production. Rice is scarce, it's going for almost $500 a ton on the world market — worth $240 or $250 — and now sometimes even with money you can't buy it. So we must work with great speed in all the rice paddies.

We are also progressing in citrus. Some solutions have appeared, and we are going to continue searching for formulas which allow us to find more jobs, more resources for the country. We have received an excellent impression from the construction workers, who were receptive to what was pointed out to them, and clear prospects can be seen in all of that.

The sugar workers have had a marvelous response, and things haᴅ also been pointed out to them. And what we wanted to say is that we can't win this battle, we can't overcome this special period if we do stupid things, or we're negligent, or we lose faith. There was really no reason why the seed banks and other things were lost, when they should have been preserved.

No hesitation discussing wages

So we have survived these years, which were hard and somewhat demoralizing. There were errors, things that were done badly, and there still are and will be in the future. But our struggle must be implacable, we must come out of this congress like a brave army, which has been able to discuss anything. There was no hesitation in discussing wages, although we know what many workers are feeling at this moment; they have needs, but less money. Now the produce is a little cheaper in the farmers' markets, but we have to work very hard so that they become even less expensive and so prices don't go up again.

We've made calculations to the point of exhaustion. It hurts us very much to know that there are sectors making a big effort without a great remuneration, such as teachers and health workers. The health and education sectors must have about 700,000 workers in diverse categories, including doctors, nurses, technicians, hospital personnel — 700,000 to 800,000 workers. A small wage rise would mean hundreds of millions of pesos more circulating each year.

We are happy to know that with the measures taken during the special period and the new forms of payment, of socialist remuneration, with the things we did in agriculture, the creation of the UBPCs and the improvements in the work of the state farms, it is possible to hear that an agricultural worker earned 11,000 pesos in one year working and producing a lot. The incomes of hundreds of thousands of agricultural workers have gone up in many cases, since they were the worst paid in the country. This was an error committed in other times, when some sectors such as agriculture had minimum wages — not so many years ago — of 80 pesos a month. This, of course, contributed to the exodus to the cities.

Now the situation has changed. It's very good news that so many thousands of people have joined the UBPCs, the state farms, the various plans, and they are building housing, sometimes from marabú, and we are producing a little more cement, a few more iron rods. Our plans to build about 50,000 low-cost housing units are being met. That wasn't a goal, it was an idea, but it spread rapidly, and we have to see how we can progress.

You saw what the members of the UBPCs in Las Tunas have done, the houses they have built, how they found ways to do things, how they have moved in. Really, what gave me a laugh was when one of them explained how he moved, even though he had a good house in town, and how the union leader and later the secretary of the party cell also moved in. That's the way to win the battle, there's no doubt about it. He did what he had to do to plant hundreds of kilometers of plants to serve as fencing when there was no wire. That's very important. To gather up all the cows running around loose and guarantee the milk for a town with hundreds of children, that's a feat, and it demonstrates what we can accomplish with what we have. If there is no fencing, there are plants, and there are many other solutions our people have come up with in these years of the special period.

We may have to erect a monument one day to the special period! If we keep on learning the way we have been learning, if two or three congresses more are like this one, we will have to start laying the cornerstone for a monument to the special period for teaching us to live off our own resources and to take much better advantage of everything we have. Our people's intelligence, knowledge and training is our invaluable treasure. How much money would the International Monetary Fund have to lend so that any other country in Latin America could have the levels of education, culture and health that Cuba has today, despite the special period? Just to do so in Latin America, that institution wouldn't have enough funds. But we have this human resource and we have to preserve it. Every day we have to find one cent more for a project which we carried out before when resources were not a problem. The limiting factor was our lack of administrative efficiency in investing and other things. Nor did we have the experience, we must admit, that we have now, in living with what we have, with what we have created, with the talent that this revolution has developed. Who knows how much more is yet to be seen, discovered and experienced. A country that has intelligence, above all, can live off its own resources. Without that, there is no escape for anybody. That does not mean that we overestimate our possibilities; we must be aware, as was mentioned here, that we must still improve.

Look how this country has progressed in medicine, which may be the area in which we have advanced the most from a scientific point of view. And who taught us? We taught ourselves. Of course, this does not mean renouncing other possibilities. If there is a new technology for widening an artery, we should use it immediately. In pediatric cardiovascular surgery there were a few foreigners who helped us — we never threw them out — but we had confidence in our medical system, in our doctors, in our scientists. We organized research centers, we purchased bibliographies, all the equipment, we built all the universities that were necessary.

We are a medical power. We are a cultural power, as a result of our modest efforts at the start of the revolution with art schools and all that. We are an educational power and we became so principally on the basis of our own experiences and our own teachers. We now have a profusion of universities. All the university-educated teachers who stayed — I'm not going to say that there are too many of them because they might feel hurt — can work and help us with their knowledge, their science.

As has been demonstrated here in this congress, we are in good shape in many things and in not-so-good shape in others. We don't have an industrial culture, although we have advanced a lot. Others have the advantage of having an industrial culture in their habits, in their respect for technical norms. We don't have a culture for administration and efficiency and we have to acquire this at all costs and develop it with all speed.

We must promote initiative

We need to promote men and women with initiative because as someone said, "Oh, if only there were 1,000 comrades like the one from Las Tunas!" I'm sure that in this country there are thousands of comrades like the one from Las Tunas, like the one from Ciego de Avila, like the one from Holguín, like the one from Guantánamo, like those from any province in the country. We have them, but we must discover them, we must promote men and women with initiative, ideas, determination, character and a vocation for dealing with people, because in the efforts talked about here, the subjective element played a very important role, winning over all of those involved.

We had an experience of the war. The war was hard, going up and down mountains is hard and the sacrifices are great. Nevertheless, many people joined such a difficult effort. We wouldn't have been able to win the war if we hadn't won over the people. Whoever wants to win a battle, to achieve an objective, must first win over the people. The moral stimulus is not only giving someone a diploma but saying "good morning," asking about the relative who is sick.

The capitalists, who exploit the workers, have studied a lot of techniques about winning the sympathy of the workers, they have really studied it. We socialists, who see work as a duty, don't concern ourselves so much about that, and in general socialists did not pay much attention to the individual. Now we are doing a much better job of combining material incentives and moral incentives. But that comrade could never have had enough money to do the things he did; it was a matter of winning over those who were going to do things with him. He even had to win over the affection of the cows, who were going to give milk to the people of Guayabal.

For a long time we were too optimistic about ideas. Moral incentives were practically the focus, and in fact we did many things with moral incentives. What our people have done is tremendous. The 500,000 citizens who have gone on internationalist missions, what have we paid them with? I say this because we cannot underestimate moral influences in the slightest, even, I repeat, wishing someone good morning. This people has done great things with moral force and moral incentives.

I think that now we are happily combining these concepts, in terms of payment for work, at least. I don't know if there is the same concern today about moral incentives as there is for material incentives, but at least in terms of ideas, in terms of concepts, we are clear that they must be combined.

I am convinced that there is no moral incentive comparable to what those comrades experienced when they spoke here explaining what they had done, the pride they felt. They are like the independence fighters. Everything they did was for honor, patriotism, pride.

Let's combine the two things: people's satisfaction with what they have done and the benefits they and their families can receive from what they have done. I think that also is an important lesson of the special period.

The path is really very clear. I don't want to fail to mention how moved I was to see all the different examples here. Permit me to say that the congress has had great moral and human value. It's almost frightening to think about that worker who turned over 71,000 pesos earned through voluntary work to defend the country. It's even a blow to the excess currency in circulation. He didn't spend it — and this is not a criticism of anyone who goes to buy anything in the farmers' markets — he turned it in. What an example!

Equally moving was that case of the woman from Holguín who turned over $16,000. And the man from Ciénaga de Zapata, who turned over $20,000. Don't you think that these examples will go down in history and symbolize this period? We're not urging other citizens to do the same, it would be inconceivable, that's not what we're asking. But you feel pride and admiration for the human species when you find people so unselfish, so generous.

We could also see a lot of feeling, a high morale in a large number of the comrades who spoke here. I could say that for every speaker in general; some were more impressive, maybe because of the ability to express what they feel inside, while the woman who donated the $16,000 didn't want to talk. She said, "I want to do more than talk." But many comrades expressed truly profound and admirable sentiments here. They are true examples for us. Knowing that there are such men and women is one more reason why all of us who have responsibilities should do our jobs better and struggle harder, because it's really worth the effort.

We can analyze calmly

It's admirable how ideas are so powerful that they can be truly invincible. That is why we can serenely and calmly view the enemy's maneuvers, what they could be thinking. Sometimes we even know what they are thinking, but we have the luxury of analyzing them calmly, serenely. We know they suffer because of what we've done, how we've stood our ground. We know it makes them furious and that rage can be dangerous.

Their country is also going through an election campaign which is madness. Politicking reigns, and that makes them dangerous. At this moment, people with the necessary character are not at the forefront. Sometimes we see symptoms of weakness which are amazing. The very fact that this administration in the end supported the cruel, inhumane, brutal and stupid Helms-Burton Act demonstrates an undeniable weakness of character and a lack of ethics.

But I didn't come here to stir you up; on the contrary, I came here to urge all of you and ourselves to be composed, patient, to combine patience with intelligence. If there is one thing our enemies should know, it was summed up once in a phrase: "Intelligence must be accompanied by valor and valor must be accompanied by intelligence." Believe in the party, in the serenity and composure of the party, because we clearly see all the maneuvers and provocations aimed at creating conflicts, if possible, since they cannot bear to see Cuba's heroic resistance. Let's say it gives them heartburn.

It seems that everything Cuba has done in these years, the trial it is going through, the successes it is beginning to have, cause very sharp chest pains and heart attacks to others. And we have such good medications for heart attacks, produced in our laboratories! Streptokinase is excellent and does not cause any clotting.

The superpower is always super-arrogant, without — I repeat — the necessary character in certain circumstances, without ethics, and this is dangerous. The revolution's goal is not to win wars. Its goal is to win a war if it is imposed on us; but we have no intention of promoting war or of being provoked.

This country's situation is far from desperate, and for that reason we are calm, hopeful, and we have no need for conflict. We can win our battles without conflict. That is, we do not want war, but no one should get the crazy idea of taking military action against Cuba, even with illusions about their technological resources. No one should get the notion that they could force this people to its knees. No one should get carried away with the notion that this country can be humbled, or that we wouldn't be able to fight for 100 years and all the years necessary.

We want and need peace in order to continue with this heroic work, but no one should get the idea of interfering with the effort we're making, or trying to destroy what we're doing. No one should get the notion of provoking us. We have accomplished feats up until now, but this people is capable of much greater feats.

This defines our policies. Our party, our country have an excellent leadership team, in the party and the government, in the CTC, in the mass organizations. We have everything necessary to achieve our objectives and we have the will to accomplish them.

We want all those millions of children to be able to benefit from what we are building today. Anyone who attacks Cuba's interests is not attacking our interests. We do not fight principally for ourselves, but for children such as the one we saw here today. We are fighting for our young people, for our students, and we want to nurture our dream that one day they can live in a country like the country we know we are capable of building. We cherish the illusion that all that hope expressed to us by our illustrious visitors will never be betrayed and that the symbol that Cuba has become will be maintained. We didn't want Cuba to become a symbol, but the symbolism stems from our duty and our need, plus our enemies' hostility and hatred of the fact that we want to do what we consider just and noble, because what we want is the best, not only for our people, but for all the peoples.

That is why we like to call ourselves internationalists, socialists, communists. And they are going to respect us more because of it, since those who betray their ideals are not respected, those who betray their principles have never been respected and will never be respected. For that reason, we are certain that Cuba will be respected, Cubans will be respected, our people will be respected.

There are three things that fortify us, which have become very clear since the Central Committee plenum and since this congress: the expression of what we have wanted to be, of what we are and of what we will always be.

Therefore, with true pride we can all say today, so that no one can doubt it:

Socialism or death!

Patria o muerte! [Homeland or death!]

Venceremos! [We will win!]

Also published by Ocean Press

ZR RIFLE
The plot to kill Kennedy and Castro
Second, expanded edition
by Claudia Furiati
Thirty years after the death of President Kennedy, Cuba has opened its secret files on the assassination, showing how and why the CIA, along with anti-Castro exiles and the Mafia, planned the conspiracy.
"Adds new pieces to the puzzle and gives us a clearer picture of what really happened." — *Oliver Stone*
ISBN 1-875284-85-0

THE CUBAN REVOLUTION AND THE UNITED STATES
A chronological history
Second, expanded edition
by Jane Franklin
An invaluable resource for scholars, teachers, journalists, legislators, and anyone interested in international relations, this volume offers an unprecedented vision of U.S.-Cuba relations. This updated, second edition includes detailed coverage of U.S.-Cuba events up to the end of 1995.

HAVANA-MIAMI
The U.S.- Cuba migration conflict
by Jesús Arboleya
This book examines the origins of the migration conflict and why it remains one of the most difficult issues in U.S.-Cuba relations.
ISBN 1-875284-91-5

ISLAND UNDER SIEGE
The U.S. blockade of Cuba
by Pedro Prada
Cuban journalist Pedro Prada presents a compelling case against this "last wall" of the Cold War, showing how the 35-year blockade has affected life in the tiny island nation.
ISBN 1-875284-88-5

Also published by Ocean Press

IN THE EYE OF THE STORM
Castro, Khrushchev, Kennedy and the Missile Crisis
by Carlos Lechuga
For the first time, Cuba's view of the most serious crisis of the Cold War is told by one the leading participants. Rushed to New York during the crisis to take up the post of Cuba's ambassador at the United Nations, Carlos Lechuga provides a coherent history of what really occurred when the world was on the edge of a nuclear catastrophe. Lechuga also reveals exclusive details of his participation in a secret dialogue between Washington and Havana immediately prior to the assassination of President Kennedy, discussions that could have led to a thaw in U.S.-Cuba relations.
ISBN 1-875284-87-7

THE SECRET WAR
CIA covert operations against Cuba, 1959-62
by Fabián Escalante
The secret war that the CIA lost. For the first time, the former head of Cuban State Security speaks out about the confrontation with U.S. intelligence and presents stunning new evidence of the conspiracy between the Mafia, the Cuban counterrevolution and the CIA. General Fabián Escalante details the CIA's operations in 1959-62, the largest-scale covert operation ever launched against another nation.
ISBN 1-875284-86-9

CIA TARGETS FIDEL
The secret assassination report
Only recently declassified and published for the first time, this secret report was prepared for the CIA on its own plots to assassinate Cuba's Fidel Castro. Under pressure in 1967 when the press were probing the alliance with the Mafia in these murderous schemes, the CIA produced this remarkably frank, single-copy report stamped "secret — eyes only." Included is an exclusive commentary by Division General Fabián Escalante, the former head of Cuba's counterintelligence body.
ISBN 1-875284-90-7

Also published by Ocean Press

FACE TO FACE WITH FIDEL CASTRO
A conversation with Tomás Borge
The issues confronting a changing world are frankly discussed in this lively dialogue between two of Latin America's most controversial political figures.
ISBN 1-875284-15-X

AFROCUBA
An anthology of Cuba writing on race, politics and culture
Edited by Pedro Pérez Sarduy and Jean Stubbs
What is it like to be Black in Cuba? Does racism exist in a revolutionary society which claims to have abolished it? How does the legacy of slavery and segregation live on in today's Cuba? *AfroCuba* looks at the Black experience in Cuba through the eyes of the island's writers, scholars and artists. The collection mixes poetry, fiction, political analysis and anthropology, producing a multi-faceted insight into Cuba's rich ethnic and cultural reality.
ISBN 1-875284-41-9

CUBA: TALKING ABOUT REVOLUTION
New, expanded edition
Conversations with Juan Antonio Blanco by Medea Benjamin
A frank discussion on the current situation in Cuba, this book presents an all-too-rare opportunity to hear the voice of one of the island's leading intellectuals. Juan Antonio Blanco considers new political and ethical issues that have arisen in Cuba in recent years.

CHE — A MEMOIR BY FIDEL CASTRO
Preface by Jesús Montané
Edited by David Deutschmann
For the first time Fidel Castro writes with candor and affection of his relationship with Ernesto Che Guevara, documenting his extraordinary bond with Cuba from the revolution's early days to the final guerrilla expeditions to Africa and Bolivia. Castro vividly portrays Che — the man, the revolutionary and the thinker — and describes in detail his last days with Che in Cuba.   ISBN 1-875284-15-X

Also published by Ocean Press

THE GREENING OF THE REVOLUTION
Cuba's experiment with organic farming
edited by Peter Rosset and Medea Benjamin
The first detailed account of Cuba's turn to a system of organic agriculture, prepared on an international scientific delegation and fact-finding mission on low-input, sustainable agriculture.
ISBN 1-875284-80-X

FIDEL AND RELIGION
A conversation with Frei Betto
Brazilian liberation theologist Frei Betto engages Fidel Castro in a fascinating conversation over 23 hours, in which they discuss his childhood and education in Jesuit schools through to his motivation in initiating the guerrilla movement which led to the revolution.

In this book, which has been a best-seller throughout Latin America, Castro speaks candidly about his views on religion and many other topics.
ISBN 1-875284-05-2

THE FERTILE PRISON
Fidel Castro in Batista's jails
by Mario Mencía
This is the story of Fidel Castro and his young comrades, including two women, when they were imprisoned after the July 26, 1953 attack on the Moncada military garrison, and how the Batista dictatorship was eventually forced to release them. Included in this volume are many documents such as Castro's letters from prison, published for the first time, as well as an extensive glossary and chronology.
ISBN 1-875284-08-7